ting Reads
hic Novels

to 16+ age range

L REGISTER

EDITOR: GEOFF DUBBER

SLA
School Library Association

SLA
School Library Association

Acknowledgements

Thanks to Bev Humphrey for reading and commenting on this text and to Richard Leveridge and Jane Cooper from the SLA Publications Team.

Published by:
School Library Association
1 Pine Court, Kembrey Park, Swindon SN2 8AD
Tel: 01793 530166 Fax: 01793 481182
Email: publications@sla.org.uk
Web: www.sla.org.uk

Registered Charity No: 313660
Charity Registered in Scotland No: SC039453

ISBN 978-1-903446-96-6

Printed by Holywell Press, Oxford

Contents

Series editor's note: The ISBN numbers given in this publication are indicative of currently available titles; other editions and formats may be available.

Introduction

Thank you for buying this Riveting Read publication from the School Library Association. In this book, I hope to provide you with some new ideas and some inspiration for what to do with graphic novels in your library. Comics and graphic novels are sort of like the 'black sheep' of the books world (certainly in this country), but there is no valid or logical reason why this should be. They are an untapped educational resource and can be invaluable in turning many children on to the joys of books and reading. As literacy facilitators, it's our job to match the right book to the right student and I don't think we can afford to ignore the potential of graphic novels to help us in achieving this.

It's difficult to make assumptions on what knowledge levels you all have when it comes to comics. Some of you will be experienced and avid comics readers. However, I suspect most of you will be very new to the medium and will look at the thousands of titles available and think 'Oh my goodness, where do I start?!' Apologies to anyone who finds some of the content of this introduction simplistic or obvious but I'm going to pitch it at those readers who I think will need the most guidance.

We should start off with a definition of terms. You may have heard terms like 'comics', 'graphic novels' and 'manga' thrown about and wondered what the actual differences are. According to Wikipedia, 'A comic book is a publication that consists of comic art in the form of sequential juxtaposed panels that represent individual scenes. Panels are often accompanied by brief descriptive prose and written narrative, usually dialogue contained in word balloons emblematic of the comic art form'. I can't deny the accuracy of that but it might not be the best description of comics to a librarian wondering what to put on his/her shelves!

In terms of actual content, comics, graphic novels and manga are essentially all the same thing. Let's try to clear this up a little though.

- **Comics** – These are short publications of usually 30–40 pages and are traditionally printed on paper (although many comics have a digital equivalent also available these days) with a slightly-thicker paper cover. Physically speaking they are comparable to most magazines and newspapers found in a newsagent's.
- **Graphic Novels** – These can often appear like larger versions of the hundreds of paperback and hardback novels you will already have on your library shelves. Some are created directly for the graphic novel format but many are collections of already published comics (see above). If individual issues of comics have sold well, they will usually be gathered together and repackaged as a graphic novel. The total number of pages in a graphic novel could be any number really but you will notice that the paper quality and the thickness of the cover (on paperbacks) will be of a higher quality.
- **Sequential Art** – You may come across this term when researching comics. It's not widely used by comics readers but is favoured by those who study comics academically. It is used to describe any form of storytelling that involves pictures or symbols or pictographs in a specific sequence.

- **Manga** – Manga is essentially Japanese comics. Most of the manga we see in this country has been translated into English by American publishers who have bought the rights to whatever series it might be. This is the strict definition of the word "manga" and shouldn't be confused with drawing in a 'manga-style' (as many Western artists do) nor with 'anime' which might share many stylistic and production similarities with manga but actually means 'animation'.
- **Bandes Dessinées** – Another term you won't see used much but it has a simple meaning. These are comics produced for the French/Belgian comics markets. The most popular examples would be *Asterix, Tintin* and *The Smurfs.*

The most important thing to remember about comics (and I include graphic novels and manga when using this term from now on) is that they are a MEDIUM and not a genre. They are a medium for telling stories and, in that sense, are no different to other storytelling media like prose novels, audiobooks, plays, movies, TV shows, etc. Comics are able to tell stories in whichever genre you can think of. When many people talk about comics they are only talking about superhero stories and so it becomes generally accepted that comics can only tell stories about superheroes. There are two very simple reasons for this – Marvel and DC. These enormous publishing companies are the biggest producers of comics in the world… and they deal almost exclusively in superhero stories. As a result, their output dominates the market and influences much of what other publishers do as well. This isn't a criticism of Marvel or DC. This is a perfectly natural business practice and something we see in plenty of other fields. Yes, 'The Big Two' dominate the comics landscape (and much of the cinematic landscape, as well) these days but this doesn't mean they can't and don't produce a number of excellent stories with excellent writing and excellent artwork. Never trust a 'Graphic Novels Recommended Reading List' that purposely ignores the output of Marvel and DC just because they are popular.

Advice

As one librarian to another, there are a few pieces of advice I offer if you are starting up or improving your own graphic novel collections:

- **Use the book-buying skills you already have** – You already buy plenty of books that you've never read (and in the case of non-fiction perhaps don't even fully understand!) but that doesn't stop you taking the plunge and getting them in. This is because you use your experience, product knowledge and best judgement. Sometimes it doesn't work but more than often it does. You can do the same with graphic novels and this Riveting Read will provide you with an excellent starting point for exploration and "plunge-taking".
- **Nobody expects you to have looked at every page** – There is an immediacy about comics and graphic novels that can cause librarians to… worry. Most of the time the content of graphic novels is no more offensive than that of regular prose fiction for children and young adults. It's just that an image leaps off the page much quicker than a paragraph of text does. This

shouldn't put you off buying them though. How many of us bought Stephenie Meyer's *Twilight* books without having read them? Again, use your judgement and your discretion. And this book.

- **Read one yourself** – Seems obvious, doesn't it? Even if the style isn't to your taste and isn't what you would normally prefer to read, give it a go. You'd be surprised how much it can increase your own knowledge of how the medium works. It gives you a greater empathy towards your own comics-reading students too. When I started work in my first school library post, I read plenty of Jacqueline Wilson novels. Why? Because they were being borrowed at a phenomenal rate and I wanted to understand why. I was glad I did too! If you've never read a graphic novel before, I'd very much recommend you do so. It doesn't have to be about The Hulk or Batman. You can choose something with more 'adult' themes that actually has a subject matter you have an interest in. The choice is yours.
- **Take part in the Excelsior Award** – The Excelsior Award (and its spin-off, the Excelsior Award Junior) is the UK's biggest book award for graphic novels where children decide the winner! Launched in 2011, it now regularly attracts over 200 schools from all the UK and provides librarians with some of the most school-friendly graphic novels in any given year. For full details, visit the site at http://www.excelsioraward.co.uk/

How to use this book

I believe that every library (both public and school) should have a well-stocked, modern, vibrant and coherent collection of graphic novels. However, I also accept that getting the most appropriate stock is not always easy. That's where this Riveting Read comes in. It provides you with over 150 different graphic novels for your consideration. I'm not suggesting that you need to buy each and every one of these in order to have the best possible collection in your library. Each library is different and caters for different children. Obviously it's down to you to decide on which (and how many) of these titles will suit your budget and your readers best.

The list is split up into four, age-appropriate sections: 8–11, 11–14, 14–16 and 16+. These are just guidelines though, not strict rules to be followed at all times. They are there to give you some advice on what age range of children might usually read them. Sometimes it's just a case of subject material and these divisions shouldn't be seen as any indicator of 'offensive content'. Personally speaking, I would say that most of the titles in the 16+ category are 'sixth form only' but there a few in there that I would (and have) loaned out to younger students in Years 10 and 11. Again, it's a question of using your judgement.

You might also notice that many of the titles are suffixed with the term 'Volume 1'. Again, this is a guideline and is meant to show you that there are further volumes available in that series should you find that your 'Volume 1' has become hugely popular.

There are a couple of notable (and major) omissions in this book – Japanese manga and *The Simpsons*. The reasons for this are as follows. Firstly, I think the field of manga is large enough and popular enough to warrant a Riveting Read of its own. Perhaps the SLA will look into this at some point in the future. There are titles from the Manga Shakespeare series in here (see the publisher's website for the full list http://www.selfmadehero.com/books.php?series=1), but these were published in Britain and employed British illustrators, so aren't 'manga' in the strictest sense of the word. Secondly, *The Simpsons* graphic novels are a no-brainer. Any and all of them would be a great addition to your library's graphic novel stock… and they would definitely get borrowed a lot.

Finally, I have added a 'rating system' for every graphic novel in this list. It's called **Lendability** and is an indicator of popularity and of how much I would expect each graphic novel to be borrowed. It is NOT meant to be seen as an indicator of quality. There are books in this Riveting Read that you should seriously consider having in your library (*Persepolis*, for example) for their critical acclaim if nothing else. However, you shouldn't expect these books to be borrowed as frequently as, say, *Avengers vs X-Men* will be. This is no different to what we do with our normal fiction sections though. Most of us will have novels by Jane Austen and Charles Dickens on our shelves but we don't expect them to be borrowed as heavily as books by Roald Dahl and J. K. Rowling. This doesn't mean we should scrap the classics – just that we should be realistic in our expectations as librarians. There are graphic novels here that I have given only 1 star (out of 4). This doesn't mean they aren't very good – it just means that most of the school are likely to have little interest in them. They could really touch the life of one child though and take their breath away… which is obviously a good thing.

I hope this Riveting Read is a fun and illuminating read for you and enables you to enter an exciting new world of literature, as well as reaching a new type of student in your schools.

Paul Register

Educational Speaker/Trainer (http://www.blokeofsteel.co.uk/)

Excelsior Award founder and organiser (http://www.excelsioraward.co.uk/)

8–11

Cover	Title	Description	Creators	Publisher	Genre	ISBN	Lendability 4 star max.
	**Adventure Time, Volume 1**	The first volume of the graphic novels based on the mega-popular and hilarious cartoon/fantasy show made for Cartoon Network. Featuring the stars of the show Finn and Jake, plus fan-favourite characters Marceline the Vampire Queen, Princess Bubblegum, Lumpy Space Princess and the Ice King!	Ryan North & Braden Lamb	Kaboom	Humour Fantasy Adventure	9781782760009	3 stars
	**Aw Yeah Comics! Volume 1: And... Action!**	It's up to Action Cat and Adventure Bug to stop the bad guys! Art Baltazar and Franco are masters at creating loveable and charming characters and presenting them in a kid-friendly and highly accessible way. This one is no exception.	Art Baltazar & Franco	Dark Horse	Action Superheroes Humour	9781616555580	3 stars
	**Batman: Li'l Gotham**	These gorgeously drawn and painted all-ages tales feature all of your favourite Gotham City characters: Batman, Robin, Nightwing, Catwoman, The Joker, The Penguin, Poison Ivy... but shrunk down into cute kiddy versions of themselves. This is a book that takes a traditionally dark subject matter (crime in Gotham City) and manages to find a lot of humour in it.	Derek Fridolfs & Dustin Nguyen	DC	Superheroes Children	9781401244941	3 stars
	**Bone, Volume 1: Out from Boneville**	Follow the adventures of the three Bone cousins – Fone, Phoney, and Smiley – as they are chased out of Boneville into a world totally alien to them and full of surprises. This is the first volume of Jeff Smith's hysterical cartoon epic and is also available in a 1,300 page collected edition.	Jeff Smith	Cartoon Books / Scholastic	Humour Adventure Fantasy	9780439706407	2 stars

	**Bunny vs. Monkey, Book 1**	*Bunny vs Monkey* is Good vs Evil and Science vs Nature. Bunny represents the rural way of life for woodland creatures. Monkey crash-lands into that life as an example of scientific endeavour out of control. This is the story of their constant and side-splitting clashes. This book won the 2015 Stan Lee Excelsior Award Junior.	Jamie Smart	David Fickling Books	Humour Animals	9781-910200070	4 stars
	**Chimichanga**	The adorable little bearded girl from Wrinkle's Traveling Circus exchanges a lock of her magic beard hair for a witch's strange egg. She then accidentally comes across upon – the savoury-named beast Chimichanga! – a fateful meeting that could save the show! This is as good an "all ages" graphic novel as you're ever likely to read. Finished runner-up in the 2012 Stan Lee Excelsior Award.	Eric Powell	Dark Horse	Humour Fantasy Adventure	9781595827555	4 stars
	**Corpse Talk, Season 1**	*Corpse Talk* is essentially a chat show that interviews famous dead people – in comic form. Blackbeard, Cleopatra, Genghis Khan, Marie Curie, Henry VIII – all are asked the questions that nobody ever got chance to ask. Witty and very informative in a *Horrible Histories* kind of way. Which is a good thing!	Adam Murphy	David Fickling Books	Factual Chat Show Humour	9781910200018	3 stars
	**Cow Boy: A Boy and his Horse**	Extremely well-presented in clear and stark panels on a black background, *Cow Boy* is the story of a young bounty hunter in the Old West who is determined to send his entire outlaw family to jail. The titular hero isn't to be messed with and yet this book has several beautiful scenes that remind you that, at his core, he's just a lonely little boy trying to do good.	Nate Cosby & Chris Eliopoulos	Archaia	Western Family Action	9781608864195	3 stars

	**Dinosaurs: In The Beginning...**	In the tradition of *Bande Dessinées* storytelling, *Dinosaurs* is a collection of short bursts of anthropomorphised prehistoric creatures living their lives and having their crazy adventures. Great for kids with short attention spans or who like dipping in and out of books.	Arnaud Plumeri & Bloz	Papercutz	Dinosaurs Humour	9781597074902	2 stars
	**Evil Emperor Penguin, Book 1**	This is... Evil Emperor Penguin! And he's plotting to TAKE OVER THE WORLD (Amazon). A humorous take on every OTT villain you might have seen in superhero comics or James Bond films.	Laura Ellen Anderson	David Fickling Books	Animals Humour	9781910200513	3 stars
	**Fantasy Sports**	Sam Bosma's debut graphic novel is almost beyond description in its extreme originality. Tomb raiding! Magic! Undead creatures, including a mummified pharaoh thing! And a game of basketball to decide the outcome of the story. Crazy but enthralling.	Sam Bosma	Nobrow	Action Adventure Sports Fantasy	9781907704802	3 stars
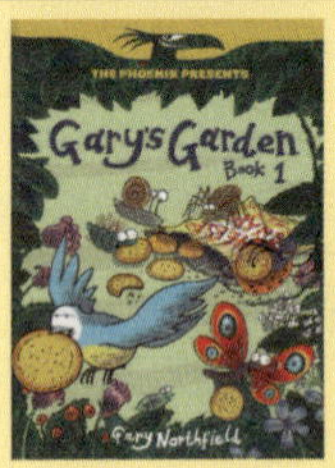	**Gary's Garden, Book 1**	Grumpy caterpillars! Space-travelling ladybirds! Ninja hedgehogs are all to be found in Gary's garden as he chills. The story of what could be happening all around you if you only knew where and when to look. Featured in *The Phoenix* weekly comic.	Gary Northfield	David Fickling Books	Humour Animals	9781910200094	3 stars

	**Hilda and The Troll**	All of Luke Pearson's *Hilda* books have been critically acclaimed and most have won prizes too – with good reason. Highly accessible and highly magical, Hilda is a little girl who goes on the most incredible adventures. This is the first book in the series and manages to feel a little European and a little Japanese at the same time. Wonderful world-building.	Luke Pearson	Flying Eye	Fantasy	9781909263789	3 stars
	**Itty Bitty Hellboy**	Art Baltazar and Franco turn their cutesy attentions to Hellboy, Mike Mignola's famous, demonic, supernatural investigator with… *Itty Bitty Hellboy*! A fun and colourful, all-ages reimagining of the critically-acclaimed comics classic.	Art Baltazar & Franco	Dark Horse	Humour Children Fantasy Demons	9781616554149	3 stars
	**Long Gone Don, Book 1**	The story of ten-year-old schoolboy Don Skelton's trip to "Broilerdoom", a version of the afterlife no-one ever warned him about, one full of crazy adventures and crazier monsters! A fantasy tale with a twist created by Robin and Lorenzo Etherington for *The Phoenix* weekly comic.	The Etherington Brothers	David Fickling Books	Adventure Fantasy Death	9781910200049	2 stars
	**My Little Pony: Friends Forever, Volume 1**	Here are some *My Little Pony* favourites featured in magical friendship tales. Applejack and Pinkie Pie enter a baking contest. The Cutie Mark Crusaders team up with Discord, Spike enlists Princess Celestia to help him find a birthday present, and finally Twilight Sparkle and Shining Armor are busy with a mysterious ghost. Due to books like this, the popular toy line and the latest TV series, *My Little Pony* is more popular as a franchise than it's ever been.	Amy Mebberson, Alex De Campi, Ted Anderson, et al	IDW	Animals Movies & TV	9781613779811	3 stars

	**My Little Pony: Friendship is Magic, Volume 1**	More favourite Ponies! Read about Twilight Sparkle, Rainbow Dash, Rarity, Fluttershy, Pinkie Pie, Applejack, and other favourite! Something's not right in the town though – some strange behavior- It's up to the Mane Six to find the source of the problem before it's too late! Clearly one for *My Little Pony* fans	Katie Cook & Andy Price	IDW	Animals Movies & TV	9781613776056	3 stars
	**Oddly Normal, Book 1**	Oddly Normal is a ten-year-old girl with pointed ears and green hair – a half-witch who will be the first to tell you that having a mother from a magical land and a father from Earth doesn't make it easy to make friends at school! Funny with a charming lead character, this is a big favourite with my eight-year-old daughter.	Otis Frampton	Image	Fantasy Monsters	9781632152268	3 stars
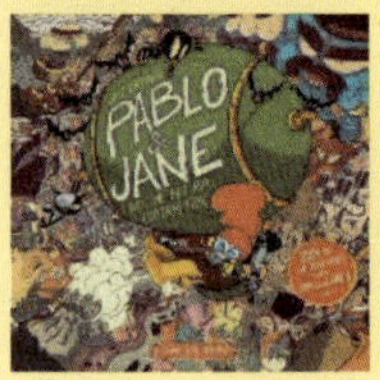	**Pablo and Jane and the Hot Air Contraption**	A strange green glow is coming from the old house up on the hill, and when Pablo and Jane decide to inquire they make an unexpected discovery! Wacky sci-fi with a couple of cute kids and lots of anthropomorphic characters, this book is something a bit different. Part story and part puzzle book with echoes of a *Where's Wally?*, this one could be very popular in a primary school classroom or library.	Jose Domingo	Flying Eye Books	Fantasy Puzzle	9781909263369	2 stars

	**Samurai Jack, Volume 1**	A big hit on Cartoon Network when he first arrived in 2001, *Jack* has found a new home in graphic novels and will appeal to readers who can appreciate a time-displaced Samurai pulled out of his historic context, into a futuristic world and given a singular quest – that of getting home and defeating the demon wizard Aku. Heavily influenced by 1970's kung-fu films and Japanese animation, this is stylish and exciting stuff.	Jim Zub & Andy Suriano	IDW	Fantasy Monsters Movies & TV	9781613778944	3 stars
	**Star Cat, Book 1**	The Star Cat is a spaceship/giant cat crewed by a Star Trek-esque collection of ridiculous bridge officers travelling the galaxy having adventures and hunting down space criminals. Another product of *The Phoenix* weekly comic. Very funny.	James Turner	David Fickling Books	Sci-fi Humour	9781910200063	3 stars
	**Teen Titans Go! Volume 1**	This series is based on the hit Cartoon Network show, but the Teen Titans themselves (in this case, the youths/sidekicks of the DC superhero universe – Robin, Cyborg, Raven, Beast Boy, Starfire) have been a regular team in DC's comics since their debut in 1964. This is kids being superheroes at their zaniest! Very cartoony!	Sholly Fisch & Ben Bates	DC	Superheroes Movies & TV	9781401252427	4 stars
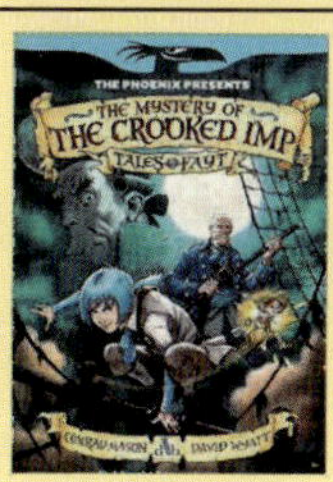	**The Mystery of the Crooked Imp**	Another product of *The Phoenix*, this is a fascinating fantasy story with a real feel of historical fiction thrown in too. Slightly reminiscent of *Peter Pan*, it's a tale of magic and fairies and kidnappings and crime fighters. Gripping adventure for higher ability readers.	Conrad Mason & David Wyatt	David Fickling Books	Fantasy Magic Crime	9781910200421	3 stars

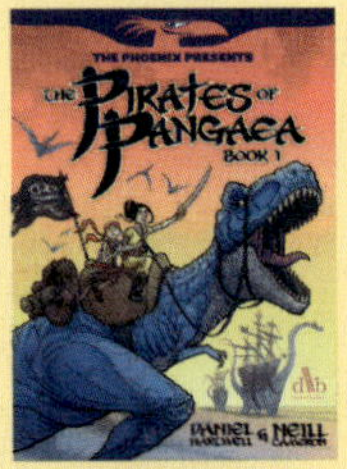	**The Pirates of Pangaea**	What do primary school children really like? Dinosaurs obviously! And pirates! So why not put both of these things in the same story?! And then add a strong female protagonist! Perfect. Excellent adventure story and beautifully drawn.	Neill Cameron & Daniel Hartwell	David Fickling Books	Adventure Dinosaurs Pirates	9781910200087	3 stars
	**Tiny Titans: Welcome to the Treehouse**	Based on the same premise as *Teen Titans Go!* (see above), Tiny Titans sees Art Baltazar and Franco bring their trademark style to the team of DC kiddy superheroes… but with a much bigger list of characters! Very much in the style of *Itty Bitty Hellboy*.	Art Baltazar & Franco	DC	Superheroes Children Humour	9781401220785	3 stars
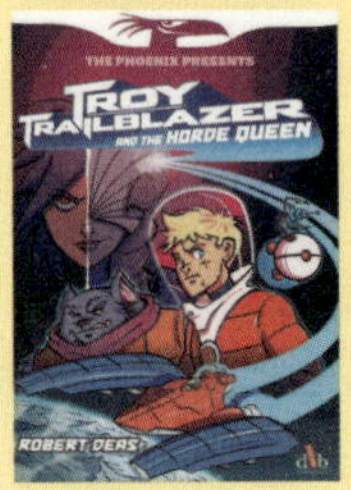	**Troy Trailblazer and the Horde Queen**	A sci-fi adventure which takes many cues from British comic strips of yesteryear like *Dan Dare*, this story features a young boy as the titular hero complete with fascinating supporting cast and heaps of added thrills for those who think travelling the galaxy and saving the universe would be a great way to live. Another story from *The Phoenix* weekly comic.	Robert Deas	David Fickling Books	Sci-fi	9781910200469	3 stars

11–14

Cover	Title	Description	Creators	Publisher	Genre	ISBN	Lendability 4 star max.
	**A Christmas Carol (Original Text)**	Graphic novel adaptation of Charles Dickens' classic tale of miserly behaviour, family togetherness and the true spirit of Christmas. Also available in *Quick Text* (ISBN 9781906332181). There is also a *Teaching Resource Pack* available (ISBN 9781907127045).	Charles Dickens & Sean Michael Wilson	Classical Comics	Classics Ghosts Literary Adaptation	9781906332174	2 stars
	**Alone, 1: The Vanishing**	A wonderful example of modern *Bandes Dessinées*. Originally published in France, this is the opening volume of the story of five children (strangers to each other, all coming from different social backgrounds) who wake up one morning to find that everybody else in their city has vanished – with no explanation as to why. They all have their own outlandish theories but the more they search for answers the more dangers they uncover. A strong mystery tale that pulls you right in and makes you experience the sense of loneliness that the main characters feel, all alone in a city made for tens of thousands.	Fabien Vehlmann & Bruno Gazzotti	Cinebook	Mystery	9781849181969	3 stars

	**Ant-Man: Second-Chance Man**	Scott Lang has never exactly been the world's best superhero. Most people don't even think he's been the best Ant-Man! He's an "everyman" figure who's been to prison and through a messy divorce. And he's been dead. But this time is different! This is a light-hearted, self-deprecating and self-conscious tale of a middle-aged superhero with no money, no clothes (apart from his Ant-Man suit!) and little future… which is why he turns down a paying job with Iron Man and relocates to Miami in an attempt to make something of himself…	Nick Spencer & Ramon Rosanas	Marvel	Superheroes Humour	9781846536649	4 stars
	**Aquaman: The Trench**	Aquaman is the King of Atlantis… but he doesn't really want to be. There's plenty of Atlanteans who don't want to see a half-human sitting on the throne too. And the humans on the surface world just see him as a joke superhero who talks to fishes and is useless out of water. Fortunately, he has a powerful Atlantean wife, Mera, who is ready to help him prove himself to the world… and to fight a terrifying new threat from the very depths of the ocean.	Geoff Johns & Ivan Reis	DC	Superheroes	9781401237103	3 stars
	**Avengers vs. X-Men**	Marvel's premier superhero teams clash in the ultimate battle for survival. Does the return of the all-powerful Phoenix entity to Earth herald the rebirth of the mutant race? That's what the X-Men believe! Unfortunately, the Avengers are convinced that the Phoenix's arrival will mean the end of all life on Earth. This is 680 pages of larger-than-life superhero battles!	Brian Michael Bendis et al	Marvel	Superheroes	9781846535185	4 stars

	**Batgirl: Batgirl of Burnside**	What is the coolest neighbourhood in Gotham? well Burnside of course! – a centre for young artists, fashionistas and techies and now Batgirl! This is Batgirl tweaked for the 21st Century, with a cool new costume, new friends, new school and new lifestyle. Ideal for readers who want to see a modern superhero story… with a traditional touchstone.	Brendan Fletcher, Cameron Stewart & Babs Tarr	DC	Superheroes	9781401257989	3 stars
	**Batman: Knightfall, Volume 1**	This was the epic 634-page story that changed Batman's status quo forever and introduced the world to the character of Bane. The inmates of Arkham Asylum have been broken out and unleashed upon Gotham City. Batman has his friends to help him (Robin, Nightwing, Batgirl) but vows to not rest until all his enemies are back in their cells. As he suffers from exhaustion and reaches breaking point, Bane makes his move… This is *Volume 1* of a long-running story and is preceded by *Volume 2: Knightquest* (ISBN 9781401235369) and *Volume 3: Knightsend* (9781401237219).	Graham Nolan et al	DC	Superheroes Crime	9781401233792	3 stars

	**Batman: The Long Halloween**	Taking place during Batman's early days of crime-fighting, this murder mystery tells the story of a killer who murders his prey only on public holidays. Batman works closely with District Attorney Harvey Dent (soon to become the psychotic Two-Face) and Lieutenant James Gordon to try and restore some notion of law and order in Gotham City… and discover the identity of "Holiday". This book was hugely influential of Christopher Nolan's *Dark Knight* trilogy of films.	Jeph Loeb & Tim Sale	DC	Superheroes Mystery Murder	9781401232597	3 stars
	**Berlin: The Seven Dwarves**	Link these two – In the year 1943, the crew of the Lancaster S-Snow White is dropping bombs on Germany and on an abandoned Lincolnshire airfield in 1993, two women exchange a 50-year-old letter and you have story. What links these women with the events of World War II? This is a highly moving tale of how young people – those in the air and those on the ground – dealt with the day-to-day realities of war, and how horror, death and love can all exist alongside each other.	Marvano	Cinebook	World War II	9781849181358	2 stars
	**Captain America: The Saga of Dimension Z**	Captain America moves from stories of international espionage to sci-fi and pulp-fantasy (with hideous monsters) and a land ruled by one of his oldest and most sadistic enemies. When he is seemingly permanently stranded in a land unrecognisable from his America, what does the Sentinel of Liberty do? What is Captain America without an America?	Rick Remender & John Romita Jr.	Marvel	Superheroes	9781846535345	3 stars

	**Captain America: Red Menace**	Captain America and SHIELD's Agent 13 stumble into the chaos of The Red Skull's legacy, as Crossbones (The Red Skull's faithful right hand) and Sin (The Red Skull's twisted daughter) clash with the criminal scientific cabal A.I.M. in America's mid-west. This book follows on from the *Winter Solider* storyline and continues Ed Brubaker's defining run on the comic.	Ed Brubaker & Steve Epting	Marvel	Superheroes Spies Espionage	9780785156178	3 stars
	**Captain America: Winter Soldier**	The movie *Captain America: The Winter Soldier* has somewhat diluted the massive shock impact this story had when it was originally published in 2006 but it still remains one of Cap's greatest ever tales as it uncovers a leftover mystery from The Cold War and puts our hero through an emotional wringer the likes of which he's rarely experienced before.	Ed Brubaker & Steve Epting	Marvel	Superheroes	9781846535796	3 stars
	**Captain Marvel: In Pursuit of Flight**	A watershed period for one of Marvel's most powerful female superheroes, writer Kelly Sue DeConnick took Carol Danvers out of the tight-fitting swimsuit and into a more traditional (and practical!) superhero costume that prepared her for her new adventures across the galaxy. She also dropped the "Ms." prefix and replaced it with the gender-neutral "Captain", thereby ushering in a new era for the character that didn't immediately focus on her supposedly being "a woman working in a man's world". A strong book for a strong character.	Kelly Sue DeConnick & Dexter Soy	Marvel	Superheroes Cosmic	9780785165491	2 stars

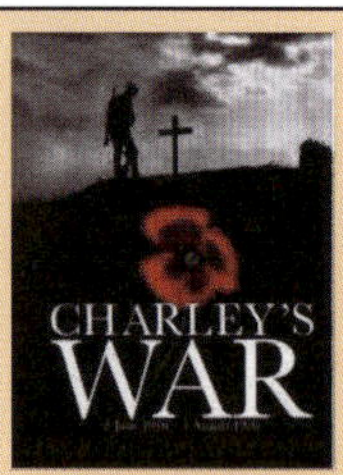	**Charley's War: 2nd June – 1st August 1916**	It is 1916, Charley Bourne is desperate to join up to serve King and Country. Like many others, he lies about his age and enlists to fight on the battlefields of France. But the seemingly needless and endless sacrifice of trench warfare sweep aside his initial thoughts of glory and patriotism. Originally published from 1979 to 1986 in comic form, this is arguably the finest work of one of *2000AD*'s primary creators Pat Mills. Still relevant today and still in publication, it is a British comics phenomenon. This is the first of ten volumes.	Pat Mills & Joe Colquhoun	Rebellion/ 2000AD	World War I	9781840236279	2 stars
	**Civil War**	The inspiration for the 2016 blockbuster Marvel movie *Captain America: Civil War*, this is the story of how one tragic accident involving reckless superheroes and a school leads to direct government intervention which demands that all superheroes register with the authorities or be declared outlaws. Captain America finds that an unacceptable infringement of his personal liberties. Iron Man thinks it makes perfect sense and that being vigilantes is no longer defendable in this day and age. Everybody else has to pick a side… and "civil war" ensues as friends have to fight friends. A powerful morality tale which makes no effort to encourage the reader to pick one side over the other and has no easy resolution.	Mark Millar & Steve McNiven	Marvel	Superheroes	9781905239603	4 stars

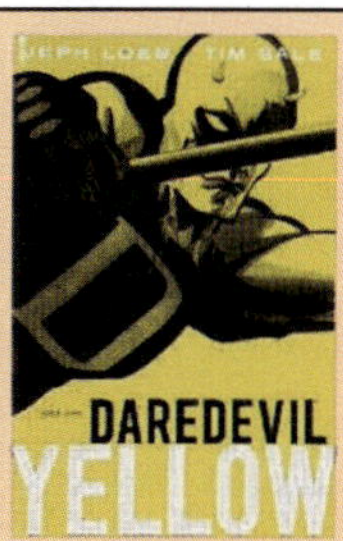	**Daredevil: Yellow**	Jeph Loeb and Tim Sale are famous for working together to tell tales of the early days of some of comics' most iconic superheroes – Spider-Man, The Hulk, Batman, Captain America. Now they turn their attentions to Daredevil and create a tale of romantic comedy that picks apart the doomed relationship of Matt Murdock (Daredevil) and Karen Page, as Matt takes his first steps into superheroics and tries to protect his friends and his home.	Jeph Loeb & Tim Sale	Marvel	Superheroes Love Loss	9780785109693	2 stars
	**Dracula (Original Text)**	A hugely faithful graphic novel adaptation of Bram Stoker's classic gothic vampire tale. Stays very close to the source material, in both style and content. Great artwork and also available in *Quick Text* version (ISBN 9781906332266).	Bram Stoker, Jason Cobley & Staz Johnson	Classical Comics	Classics Gothic Horror Literary Adaptation	9781906332259	2 stars
	**Earth 2: The Gathering**	*Earth 2* won the 2014 Stan Lee Excelsior Award with the highest score of any shortlisted book ever. Don't let the cover fool you (although it did also win the JABBICA, the award for graphic novel covers voted for by librarians) – this is the story of an alternate Earth where Batman, Wonder Woman and Superman are all killed in an alien invasion in the first dozen pages! The real story is that of the new heroes that rise when Earth is next threatened. Different heroes for a different world.	James Robinson & Nicola Scott	DC	Superheroes Parallel Worlds	9781401242817	3 stars

	**Fantastic Four, Volume 1**	The first of four volumes of Marvel's "first family" (and that is meant in a royal sense!) by sensational writer Jonathan Hickman. High adventure whilst raising a family and using every aspect of known (and sometimes unknown) science to fix the world and quite literally "solve everything".	Jonathan Hickman & Dale Eaglesham	Marvel	Superheroes Family	9780785136880	2 stars
	**Flashpoint**	Dead family members are alive, loved ones are strangers, and close friends are different, gone or worse. What has happened? The Flash has woken at his desk to find the world has changed. Who's altered the timeline but allowed him to remember the way things were? And why? This was the time-altering storyline that allowed DC Comics to reinvent their continuity and present fresh and modernised versions of their characters in *The New 52*, a publishing strategy that allowed them to "reboot" all their monthly comic titles.	Geoff Johns & Andy Kubert	DC	Superheroes Time travel	9781401233389	3 stars
	**Frankenstein (Original Text)**	Frankenstein is a classic of course and true to the original novel, Declan Shalvey's naturally gothic artistic style is a perfect match for this epic tale. This is a story of alienation, empathy and understanding beyond appearance. Also available in *Quick Text* (ISBN 9781906332167).	Mary Shelley, Jason Cobley & Declan Shalvey	Classical Comics	Classics Gothic Horror Literary Adaptations	9781906332150	2 stars

	**Green Lantern: Rebirth**	The classic tale of how writer and DC Comics' Chief Creative Officer Geoff Johns was able to reinvent Green Lantern for a new generation without undoing any of his past. Very clever and uplifting, it took Hal Jordan (Green Lantern) from the depths of his own personal despair and allowed him to be a hero again. Great supporting cast and great villains too.	Geoff Johns & Ethan Van Sciver	DC	Superheroes Redemption Cosmic	9781401227555	3 stars
	**Green Lantern: Secret Origin**	Before he became the Green Lantern of Earth, Hal Jordan was just a washed-up test pilot with no way to fly... until the dying alien Abin Sur granted him his power ring, one of the most powerful weapons in the universe. Geoff Johns brings you the life story of Hal Jordan and sets in motion all the tales he wanted to tell over the coming years. Not a traditional superhero story by any means, this deals with the concept of being human first (and part of a family) and being an intergalactic cop second.	Geoff Johns & Ivan Reis	DC	Superheroes Aliens Sci-fi	9781401230869	3 stars
	**Green Lantern: Sinestro Corps War**	In response to the very existence of the Green Lanterns Corps across the galaxy, Sinestro – Hal Jordan's former mentor and arch-nemesis – forms his own corps of "volunteers" and attacks Earth with an army of soldiers fuelled by the fear they instil in others! An exciting and gorgeously rendered, big, thick, superhero battle book!	Geoff Johns et al	DC	Superheroes Battles	9781401233013	3 stars

	**Groo: The Hogs of Horder**	Making his first appearance in 1982, Groo the Wanderer is the creation of Spanish cartoonist Sergio Aragonés (also famous for his work on *Mad Magazine* and for his somewhat indirect and accidental contribution to the death of Marty Feldman. See https://en.wikipedia.org/wiki/Sergio_Aragonés A humorous version of *Conan the Barbarian*, Groo is as skilled a swordsman as he is completely stupid. *Groo* was one of the first widely successful creator-owned comics and is still one of the few successful humorous comic books in the United States.	Sergio Aragonés & Mark Evanier	Dark Horse	Humour Cartoons Fantasy	9781595824233	2 stars
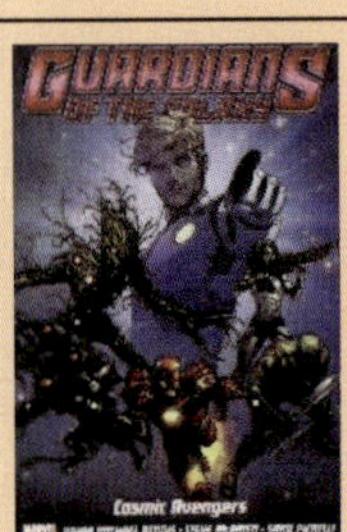	**Guardians of the Galaxy, Volume 1: Cosmic Avengers**	There's a new rule in the galaxy: no one touches Earth! Why has Earth become so important? That's what the Guardians of the Galaxy are going to find out! Iron Man joins the team made famous in the 2014 Marvel movie as they defend Earth from all manner of intergalactic dangers.	Brian Michael Bendis & Steve McNiven	Marvel	Superheroes Cosmic	9781846535420	4 stars
	**Guardians of the Galaxy: The Complete Collection, Volume 1**	Led by Star-Lord, the new Guardians of the Galaxy include a who's who of the mightiest – and most bizarre – protectors the stars have ever seen! Rocket Raccoon, Drax the Destroyer, Groot, Gamora, Adam Warlock, Mantis, the all-new Quasar, Cosmo the telepathic space dog and more take on the universe's most dangerous menaces – and have fun while doing it! The primary influence for the massively successful 2014 *Guardians of the Galaxy* movie, this first volume from British writing team Dan Abnett and Andy Lanning has all the requisite humour mixed with mind-blowing cosmic adventures that fans of the film would expect from a *Guardians* graphic novel. Good value for money.	Dan Abnett, Andy Lanning & Paul Pelletier	Marvel	Superheroes Sci-fi Cosmic	9780785190646	3 stars

	**Hulk: Gray**	Another Loeb and Sale collaboration that sees Bruce Banner recounting his first few days as The Hulk to his therapist. Sad, tragic and haunting, *Hulk: Gray* moves beyond the *Frankenstein*-esque stories of an angry monster smashing stuff and gets to the heart of the shattered life of Bruce Banner.	Jeph Loeb & Tim Sale	Marvel	Superheroes	9780785113461	3 stars
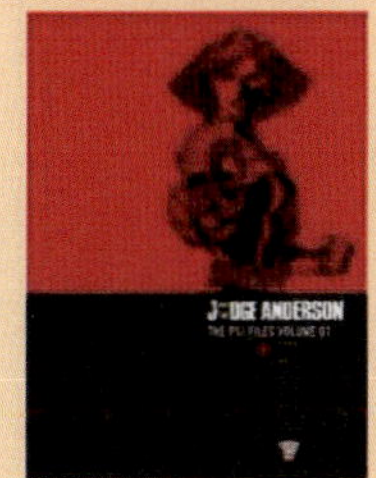	**Judge Anderson: Psi Files, Volume 1**	Originally a popular spin-off from the pages of *Judge Dredd*, Judge Cassandra Anderson of Mega-City One's Psi-Division carved a strong niche for herself in the pages of British sci-fi weekly comic 2000AD. As a precognitive telepath and empath, *Judge Anderson*'s writers were able to tell stories that, whilst still contained in the future police state of Mega-City One, dealt with the paranormal and the supernatural in a way that Judge Dredd stories couldn't. 300 pages including bonus material.	John Wagner, Alan Grant, et al	Rebellion/ 2000AD	Sci-fi Crime Dystopia	9781906735227	2 stars
	**Judge Dredd Case Files 1**	Since his debut in the second issue of *2000AD* in 1977,Judge Dredd has become a dominant force in the British comic scene. He is judge, jury and executioner, a merciless far-future lawman delivering swift justice on the streets of Mega-City One. Dredd is one of the few characters in comics who has aged in real time (meaning he is now nearly 30 years older than he was in his first comic appearance) and the *Judge Dredd Case Files* tell his full story in chronological order! And if you find that Volume 1 is popular in your library, there's plenty more material to supplement it – Volume 27 appeared in the summer of 2016	John Wagner, Carlos Ezquerra, et al	Rebellion/ 2000AD	Sci-fi Crime Dystopia	9781904265795	2 stars

	**Judge Dredd: The Dark Judges**	They came from Deadworld – twisted, evil versions of Mega-City One Judges with frightening supernatural powers! Led by the cadaverous super-fiend Judge Death, Judges Fear, Fire and Mortis share a chilling ethos – as only the living can break the law, all life is a crime… including everyone in Mega-City One! Only Judge Dredd and Psi-Division's finest telepath Cassandra Anderson can stop them from committing a Mega-City massacre! A more pocket-sized, "bargain" reprint edition of the classic Judge Dredd story, this is notable for some stunning black-and-white artwork by Brian Bolland.	John Wagner, Brian Bolland, et al	Rebellion/ 2000AD	Sci-fi Crime Dystopia Horror	9781781080450	3 stars
	**Judge Dredd: The Judge Child**	Another reprint edition like *The Dark Judges*, this story takes Judge Dredd from the familiar, crime-filled streets of his immense, future city and puts him on a quest to find a child who may have the power to prevent a prophesied apocalypse. His quest will take him through the irradiated wastelands of the Cursed Earth and into the very depths of uncharted space.	John Wagner, Mick McMahon, et al	Rebellion/ 2000AD	Sci-fi Crime Dystopia	9781781080085	2 stars

	**Justice League: Origin**	The flagship title of DC Comics' line-wide reboot in 2011 (known as *The New 52*), *Justice League* isn't just another superhero team origin story. It features new, modernised versions of Superman, Batman, Wonder Woman, The Flash, Green Lantern, Cyborg and Aquaman… and has them meet for the first time to save Earth from a massive alien invasion (the same alien invasion that can also be seen taking place in the *Earth 2* graphic novel covered earlier in this list… with different results). DC gave the project to their safest hands, in writer Geoff Johns and artist Jim Lee, two of the most respected creators in comics today.	Geoff Johns & Jim Lee	DC	Superheroes	9781401237882	4 stars
	**Kanan: The Last Padawan**	In the Disney XD, animated show *Star Wars: Rebels*, Kanan Jarrus is a cocky, sarcastic renegade alongside the ragtag crew of The Ghost, pitting their wits against the Galactic Empire. In times past, at the height of the Clone Wars, he was a Padawan learner, a Jedi in training. How did Kanan escape the catastrophic and murderous Jedi purge shown in the movie *Star Wars: Episode III – Revenge of the Sith*? One of the many stories set between Episodes III and IV of *Star Wars*.	Greg Weisman & Pepe Larraz	Marvel	Sci-fi Fantasy Movies & TV	9780785193661	3 stars
	**Legendary Star-Lord, Volume 1: Face it, I Rule**	The solo adventures of Peter Quill AKA Star-Lord, the star of the 2014 Marvel movie *Guardians of the Galaxy*. Full of the sort of spacey, aliens-filled, sci-fi fun and excitement as you'd expect from a *Guardians* book!	Sam Humphries & Paco Medina	Marvel	Sci-fi Superheroes Cosmic	9780785191599	4 stars

	**Long John Silver: Volume 1 – Lady Vivian Hastings**	Lady Vivian Hastings' hated husband has sent word from the Amazon: He has found the fabled city of Guiana-Capac, and his brother is to sell the entire domain to pay for an expedition, dispossessing Vivian in the process. So the lady has come to seek the one man who can help her: Long John Silver. Set twenty years after the events of *Treasure Island*, this is a stylish and (more or less) historically accurate sequel to Robert Louis Stevenson's pirate classic. A *Bandes Dessinées* title originally published in French it has been translated by Canterbury-based publisher Cinebook. There are four volumes in the series.	Xavier Dorison & Matthieu Lauffray	Cinebook	Classics Pirates Historical Fiction	9781849180627	3 stars
	**Lumberjanes: Beware the Kitten Holy**	Similar in style and tone to *Adventure Time*, *Lumberjanes* is one of those ultra-modern, ultra-fun, ultra-optimistic comic book series that celebrates life, people and the world… and appeals to comics fans both young and old. Critically acclaimed.	Noelle Stevenson, Shannon Watters, Grace Ellis & Brooke Allen	Boom!	Action Comedy	9781608866878	3 stars

	**Marineman: A Matter of Life and Depth**	A marine biologist and TV presenter; a man blessed with good looks, a good job, a good circle of friends and a life many would aspire to. But Steve Ocean also has a secret – a secret, which, if revealed, could throw his whole life into disarray! As perfect an example of an "all ages" graphic novel as you are likely to find, Marineman educates about ocean life as much as it entertains and excites. Taking influences from Aquaman, James Bond and even Steve Irwin, this is great stuff for teens.	Ian Churchill	Image	Superheroes	9781607063995	2 stars
	**Ms. Marvel, Volume 1: No Normal**	When Marvel introduced Kamala Khan (the new Ms. Marvel) to their superhero universe in 2014, the cultural impact of putting out a new comic book featuring a Muslim girl from New Jersey (and written by a Muslim woman) couldn't be overstated. And the best thing? It was actually very good too. Since then, Kamala has become a symbol of everything comics publishers are doing to increase diversity amongst their characters… and their staff too.	G. Willow Wilson & Adrian Alphona	Marvel	Superheroes	9780785190219	4 stars

	**Mudman, Volume 1**	It's the first day back at school for Owen Craig, and it's not going too well. He's been run over, got detention, and his police officer father has been taken prisoner by armed bank robbers. And now his body seems to be turning to mud! Written and drawn by Brit Paul Grist, *Mudman* has the sort of schoolboy comedy you might find in a Roald Dahl novel and remains a cult classic that exceeded all expectations.	Paul Grist	Image	Superheroes School Life	9781607065807	2 stars
	**Muhammad Ali: The King of the Ring**	Indian publisher Campfire produce a fine selection of graphic biographies and their *Muhammad Ali* one is certainly a highlight. Visit their website for the full range (including samples) at www.campfire.co.in/. All of these can be purchased in the UK through most library book suppliers and comic book stores.	Lewis Helfand & Lalit Kumar Sharma	Campfire	Sports Biography	9789380741048	3 stars
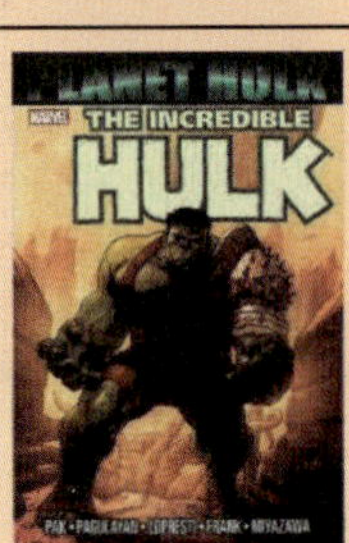	**Planet Hulk**	After an unfortunate rampage in Las Vegas, a small group of Bruce Banner's superhero friends decide that The Hulk has become far too dangerous to civilians… and trick him into boarding a rocket and being shot into deep space. The idea is that he can live out his life peacefully on an uninhabited planet. Something goes wrong though and he ends up on a savage, alien world that is ruled over by an oppressive tyrant who forces monsters like The Hulk to fight gladiatorial combats in his arena. And that's just the start of the story. And the tragedy.	Greg Pak & Carlo Pagulayan	Marvel	Superheroes Fantasy	9780785120124	4 stars

	**Robo-Hunter: The Droid Files, Volume 1**	Sam Slade is a Robo-Hunter… and one of the best in the business. Whether dealing with rebellious robots on Verdus, the sneaky mafia God-Droid and his plans to replace key human officials with robot replicas, or simply being hindered by his idiot, kit-built, robot assistant Hoagy, trouble is never far away! A bounty hunter and a detective, Sam Slade was based on the sort of hard-boiled, noir, detective fiction of 1930s America. Another veteran of *2000AD*, *Robo-Hunter* has a lot of style and attitude.	John Wagner, Alan Grant & Ian Gibson	Rebellion/ 2000AD	Sci-fi Robots	9781906735210	2 stars
	**Rocket Raccoon, Volume 1: A Chasing Tale**	Featuring the bad-tempered, mouthy, gun-toting, breakout star of the *Guardians of the Galaxy* movie, *Rocket Raccoon* is a mystery story littered with firefights, scraps and car chases across a wonderfully bright and lushly coloured galaxy. Skottie Young brings his popular and cartoony style to Rocket (and his partner Groot) and makes him more loveable than ever. And yes, he was named after the Beatles song!	Skottie Young & Jake Parker	Marvel	Sci-fi Cosmic Humour	9781846536335	4 stars

	**Rogue Trooper: Welcome to Nu-Earth**	Nu-Earth, a battle-ravaged world, forever scarred by an ongoing war. The poisonous atmosphere makes it hostile to all who fight there, with the exception of one person – Rogue Trooper. A biologically-engineered soldier, Rogue is searching for the traitor responsible for the deaths of his clone brothers... Another classic from 2000AD's 1980s period, this features amazing black-and-white artwork from Cam Kennedy and Comics Laureate Dave Gibbons.	Gerry Finley-Day, Dave Gibbons & Cam Kennedy	Rebellion/ 2000AD	Sci-fi War	9781781081136	2 stars
	**Secret Invasion**	The Skrulls, an alien race, has quietly infiltrated every super-powered organisation on Earth. They have one aim – a full scale invasion! Marvel's greatest heroes and villains must ask: Who do we trust given all the confusion & subterfuge? A typical "crossover" Marvel event book that includes nearly all their collection of superheroes, this one is gripping and better than many similar events.	Brian Michael Bendis & Leinil Francis Yu	Marvel	Superheroes Aliens	9781846534058	4 stars

	**Silver Surfer: New Dawn**	A stunning graphic novel to look at that harks back to the Silver Surfer's heyday in the sixties and early seventies. Full of multi-coloured psychedelic imagery, this is the story of one man who can travel the cosmos whenever he wants… and his new relationship with the Earth woman who keeps him grounded. Writer Dan Slott is a huge *Doctor Who* fan and the positive influence of that shines through this series.	Dan Slott & Mike Allred	Marvel	Sci-fi Cosmic Humour	9780785188780	3 stars
	**Sita: Daughter of the Earth**	Part of publisher Campfire's range of adaptations of Indian mythical epics, *Sita: Daughter of the Earth* is a beautiful book that succeeds in making a foreign culture accessible for all. Great story too.	Saraswati Nagpal & Manikandan	Campfire	Mythology	9789380741253	1 star
	**Star Wars, Volume 1: Skywalker Strikes**	The flagship title of Marvel's new *Star Wars* line of comics, this works hard to achieve the feel and look of George Lucas' original film trilogy. Luke Skywalker and the ragtag rebel band enemies of the Galactic Empire have achieved their biggest victory to date – the destruction of the massive Death Star. But the Empire's not toppled yet!... And this publication definitely succeeds. Marvel only puts its best creators on this book. If you like *Star Wars*, then you will like this comic book series too.	Jason Aaron & John Cassaday	Marvel	Sci-fi Fantasy Movies & TV	9780785192138	4 stars

	**Star Wars: Darth Vader, Volume 1: Vader**	Set between Episodes IV *(A New Hope)* and V *(The Empire Strikes Back)*, this continues the story of Darth Vader after he survives the destruction of the Death Star and finds his relationship with The Emperor strained. Another pair of excellent comics creators work on this series and it is certainly a worthy addition to the *Star Wars* canon. Full of treachery, mistrust and secret machinations.	Kieron Gillen & Salvador Larocca	Marvel	Sci-fi Fantasy Movies & TV	9780785192558	4 stars
	**Star Wars: Lando**	Another entry in Marvel's *Star Wars* line that shows readers the stories just behind the main stories. Lando Calrissian (the administrator of Cloud City in *The Empire Strikes Back*) gets himself involved in a heist and steals the one ship in all the galaxy that he really shouldn't steal. Written by Charles Soule (who won the 2015 Stan Lee Excelsior Award for his work on *Superman/Wonder Woman*) with atmospheric artwork from Alex Maleev, this is a self-contained *Star Wars* story that will be a favourite for all fans of the original trilogy.	Charles Soule & Alex Maleev	Marvel	Sci-fi Fantasy Crime Movies & TV	9780785193197	3 stars

	**Star Wars: Princess Leia**	In *Star Wars*, Princess Leia Organa witnessed the complete destruction of her homeworld, Alderaan. When her rescue came, Leia joined the Rebel Alliance in their fight to destroy the Death Star! But in the aftermath of that victory, the question remains... what is a princess without a world? And did anyone survive?... Mark Waid is one of the most reliable writers in comics and Terry Dodson provides solid and purposeful artwork without worrying about making Leia look photo-realistic. Another impressive new *Star Wars* book from Marvel.	Mark Waid & Terry Dodson	Marvel	Sci-fi Fantasy Movies & TV	9780785193173	3 stars
	**Star Wars: The Old Republic**	Set approximately 3,600 years before the movies, this publication considers the condition of the *Star Wars* galaxy in the distant past in this first volume of an “Epic Collection” series focusing on the ancient Knights of the Old Republic. Jedi, Sith, Mandalorians – they’re all here in their thousands. A fascinating look at the wider history of the *Star Wars* universe and utterly engrossing for true fans.	John Jackson Miller & Brian Ching	Marvel	Sci-fi Fantasy Movies & TV	9780785197171	3 stars

	**Supergirl: Last Daughter of Krypton**	Shot into space to escape the destruction of her homeworld Krypton at the same time as her cousin Superman, Kara Zor-el (Supergirl) has a very different introduction to Earth. Her last memory is of babysitting for her new baby cousin Kal-el (the future Superman) – so who is this mystery man in the same uniform as her, claiming to be Kal-el?! And why has she got such extraordinary new powers?! This is a new Supergirl ideal for readers who've never experienced her before – a teenage girl, scared, lost and angry, and just as powerful as Superman! This title won the 2013 Stan Lee Excelsior Award.	Mike Johnson, Michael Green & Mahmud Asrar	DC	Superheroes	9781401236809	3 stars
	**Superior Spider-Man, Volume 1 (Oversized)**	It's the story that turned Spider-Man's world upside-down, as a dying Doctor Octopus hatches his master plan for vengeance against Peter Parker... by swapping bodies with him! As Spidey finds himself trapped in an old man's dying body, Octopus vows to change his evil ways and sets himself on a new path, one of heroism. However, his real motivation is part of his revenge – to become a better Spider-Man than the original ever was and prove himself "Superior"!	Dan Slott & Humberto Ramos	Marvel	Superheroes Death	9780785185215	3 stars

	**Superman For All Seasons**	Viewed by many as Jeph Loeb's and Tim Sale's finest work together, *Superman For All Seasons* is an emotional and insightful examination of Clark Kent's transformation from a powerful boy into a heroic man. Told through the course of four seasons in the Man of Steel's adolescent life, this coming-of-age tale humanises the alien from another planet so that he is not only realistic but also relatable. Loeb and Sale show us that it is the man, not the powers, that make Clark Kent a true hero. Excellent stuff. Well worth a read. A real favourite with Superman fans.	Jeph Loeb & Tim Sale	DC	Superheroes Growing Up Family	9781563895296	2 stars
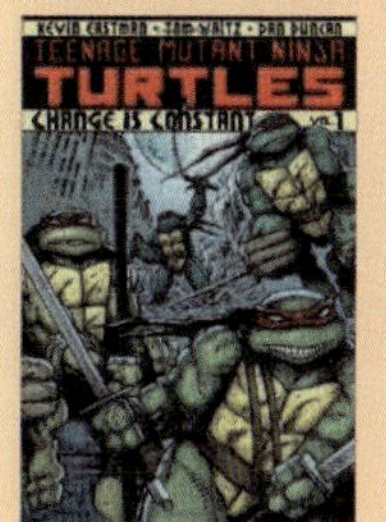	**Teenage Mutant Ninja Turtles, Volume 1: Change is Constant**	A cleverly-handled reboot for the *Teenage Mutant Ninja Turtles* as the book's creative team eschew the excessive commercial exploitation of the past and reconnect the Turtles with their grimy, indie publishing origins. This series has more in common with titles like *Batman* and *Daredevil* than the goofy, comedic cartoons of the 1990s. Finished runner-up in the 2013 Stan Lee Excelsior Award.	Kevin Eastman, Tom Waltz & Dan Duncan	IDW	Action Animals Movies & TV	9781613771396	3 stars

	**The Complete ElfQuest, Volume 1**	Discover the legendary *ElfQuest!* In an ancient fantasy setting, Elves lead a scattered existence in different tribes – Wolfriders, Sun Folk, Gliders. As these disparate groups discover each other, they are driven to try and find what their place in the world is, what their history is and why the Humans hate them so. And then there's the Trolls as well! An epic fantasy adventure that was begun in 1978 and continues to this day, the whole series can be read for free online at the creators' own website http://elfquest.com/	Wendy Pini & Richard Pini	Dark Horse	Fantasy	9781616554071	2 stars
	**The Death of Superman**	When a hulking monster emerges from an underground resting place and begins a mindless rampage, the Justice League is quickly called in to stop the colossal force of nature. But it soon becomes apparent that only Superman can stand against the monstrosity that has been nicknamed Doomsday. A story that caught the attention and the imagination of the world when it was first published in 1992, it is a tale of ultimate sacrifice and heroism and not just the superhero equivalent of heavyweight boxing. It was immediately followed by the *Funeral for a Friend* and *Reign of the Supermen* storylines.	Dan Jurgens	DC	Superheroes	9781401241827	4 stars

	**The Flash, Volume 1: Move Forward**	Currently more popular than ever due to *The Flash* TV series on Sky One, this was the first volume of his adventures as part of the 2011 DC Comics reboot (The New 52). Boasting some incredibly inventive artwork, this new series showed The Flash how vital it was for him to teach his brain to work as fast as his body. Excellent starting point for readers new to *The Flash*.	Francis Manapul & Brian Buccellato	DC	Superheroes	9781401235543	4 stars
	**The Flash: Rebirth**	A stunning, lightning-infused epic that reintroduces Barry Allen as The Flash after an absence of nearly 20 years (that's 20 years in OUR time!). How will this greatest of all Flashes deal with his resurrection and find his place in the 21st century? This graphic novel starts slowly but then quickly moves into top gear and holds that frenetic pace for most of the story. Breath-taking stuff.	Geoff Johns & Ethan Van Sciver	DC	Superheroes Resurrection	9781401230012	4 stars
	**The Hobbit**	Illustrated and hand-painted in full colour throughout, and accompanied by the carefully abridged text of the original novel, this wonderful version of JRR Tolkien's classic fantasy quest tale is a much more accurate adaptation than the movies!	JRR Tolkien & David Wenzel	Harper Collins	Fantasy Classics Literary Adaptation	9780261102668	3 stars
	**The Jungle Book**	Rudyard Kipling's classic of children's literature gets the graphic novel treatment from Indian publisher Campfire. Remains very close to the story of the original book and manages to retain the magic of the musical Disney adaptation. Highly accessible for all ages.	Rudyard Kipling, Dan Johnson & Amit Tayal	Campfire	Classics Literary Adaptation Animals	9788190751544	2 stars

	**The Kaurava Empire, Volume 1**	A space-age reimagining of one of the Sanskrit epics of ancient India. The Kauravas and Pandavas go high-tech as their forces clash in the fiercest battle the universe has ever seen (known as the Kurukshetra War in the original *Mahabharata*). Told through the eyes of the Pandava Prince and the Kaurava Prince who ultimately kills him, this tale of teenage heroism, sacrifice and adventure has been thrilling readers for centuries and propels a famous myth into the far future.	Jason Quinn & Sachin Nagar	Campfire	Mythology Sci-fi	9789380741895	2 stars
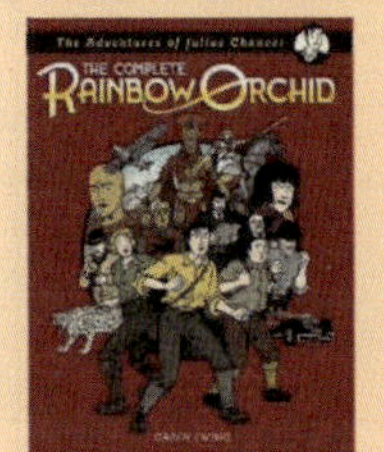	**The Rainbow Orchid**	Julius Chancer embarks on a hazardous quest for the Rainbow Orchid – a mythical flower last mentioned by the ancient Greek philosopher, Theophrastus, and steeped in legend. Ideal for anyone who enjoys historical adventure in the 1920s and the tales of *Tintin* done in a very British style.	Garen Ewing	Egmont	Adventure Historical Fiction	9781405263856	2 stars
	**The Unbeatable Squirrel Girl, Volume 1: Squirrel Power**	A comical and irreverent superhero story featuring a girl with the whackiest power-set you've ever seen – and her attempts at settling into her new college life. Squirrel Girl frequently links in with more traditional Marvel superheroes. A great read for teenage girls and loved by many men too.	Ryan North & Erica Henderson	Marvel	Superheroes School Life Humour	9780785197027	3 stars

	**Twilight: The Graphic Novel (Collector's Edition)**	Beautiful graphic novel adaptation of Stephenie Meyer's first *Twilight* book. Limited use of colour throughout and an attention to the details of Bella and Edward (particularly hair and clothes) sets this apart from other graphic novels you may have on your shelves. Definitely based on the books and not on the films.	Stephenie Meyer & Young Kim	Yen Press	Supernatural Love Vampires	9780316217170	4 stars
	**X-Men: Days of Future Past**	Originally published in comic form in 1981, this is the legendary first journey into the dystopian future of 2013 – where Sentinels stalk the Earth, most superheroes have been wiped out and the mutant population is held in internment camps. One of these mutants – a former X-Man – travels back in time in order to prevent the assassination that will cause the anti-mutant hysteria that leads to her disastrous future world.	Chris Claremont & John Byrne	Marvel	Superheroes Dystopia	9780785164531	4 stars
	**X-Men: Messiah Complex**	A race against time by a variety of factions – some pro-mutant and some anti-mutant – to capture the baby who is the first newborn mutant in years. The X-Men see this child as the key to rebuilding their depleted race... and the Marauders and the Purifiers want to see mutants extinct. Shocks aplenty at the end and a cracking X-Men story.	Various	Marvel	Superheroes	9780785123200	3 stars

14–16

Cover	Title	Description	Creators	Publisher	Genre	ISBN	Lendability 4 stars max.
	**47 Ronin**	Japan's enduring national legend comes to comics! The tale of the *47 Ronin* and their epic mission to avenge their wronged master epitomises the samurai code of honour, and creators Mike Richardson and Stan Sakai have done justice to their story! It is said that to understand the story of the *47 Ronin* is to understand Japan itself. Meticulously researched and beautifully illustrated. Hardcover edition.	Mike Richardson & Stan Sakai	Dark Horse	Legends Historical Fiction	9781595829542	2 stars
	**A Midsummer Night's Dream (Original Text)**	The entire Shakespeare play – unabridged! With its mix of real people who stumble into a fairy kingdom (with its own problems!), it's little wonder that this play is one of the best loved and most performed of all Shakespeare's masterpieces. Also available in *Plain Text* (ISBN 978-1-906332-90-7) and *Quick Text* (ISBN 978-1-906332-91-4) versions.	William Shakespeare & Jason Cardy	Classical Comics	Literary Adaptation Comedy Classics Fantasy	9781906332891	2 stars

	**ABC Warriors: The Volgan War, Volume 1**	The ABC Warriors are a battle-hardened and experienced cadre of robots first introduced in *2000AD* in 1979. In this volume they travel across Mars to recruit their latest companion, recalling as they go their battles a vicious conflict fought for oil on Earth – the Volgan War. Hammerstein, Mongrol and Joe Pineapples relate their personal experiences of fighting the bloodthirsty Ikon, and find that their tales contain a sinister common thread. Zippo & Phoenix Programm what are they all about? Written by original series creator Pat Mills, this modern take features photo-realistic, digital artwork by Clint Langley, an approach that works incredibly well with battle robots!	Pat Mills & Clint Langley	Rebellion/ 2000AD	Sci-fi War	9781907992650	3 stars
	**Alien vs Predator: Three World War**	It's decision time! A long-lost Predator clan takes on its rival clan who have been age old enemies of Earth. Earthmen must now side with the warriors who have relentlessly hunted them... but are they allies of convenience waiting their turn to strike or does the new friendship run deeper? The mystique and appeal of both the *Predator* and *Aliens* franchises continues to draw in new readers as well as appeal to seasoned fans.	Randy Stradley & Rick Leonardi	Dark Horse	Sci-fi Horror Movies & TV	9781595827029	3 stars

	**Aliens Omnibus, Volume 1**	Dark Horse took the comics industry by storm with its first *Aliens* comics in 1988, a series that truly captured the intense feel of the films it was based upon. This value-for-money, 400-page omnibus edition features the first three Dark Horse *Aliens* series – *Outbreak*, *Nightmare Asylum* and *Female War* in full colour.	Mark Verheiden et al	Dark Horse	Sci-fi Horror Movies & TV	9781593077273	3 stars
	**Aliens vs Predator Omnibus, Volume 1**	Mankind's two ultimate nightmares come together in mortal combat, and whoever wins – we lose. On the remote planet Ryushi, a small ranching community becomes an unwilling participant in a deadly ritual: extraterrestrial Predators have seeded Ryushi with Alien eggs in order to create the ultimate hunt. But what the Predators don't know is that an Alien queen egg is amongst those they've sent as potential hunting stock. This comic series from publisher Dark Horse tapped into the enduring popularity of the *Aliens* and *Predator* franchises and provided the direct impetus for Hollywood to make its own *Aliens vs Predator* movie.	Various	Dark Horse	Sci-fi Horror Movies & TV	9781593077358	3 stars
	**Amazing Spider-Man: Family Business**	A special and beautifully painted *Spider-Man* story that spans the globe and introduces readers to the sister that they (and Peter Parker!) never knew Spider-Man had! Will this sister end up becoming his greatest ally or the one who damns him? And what does The Kingpin have to do with it all?	Mark Waid, James Robinson & Gabriele Dell'Otto	Marvel	Superheroes Family	9780785184409	3 stars

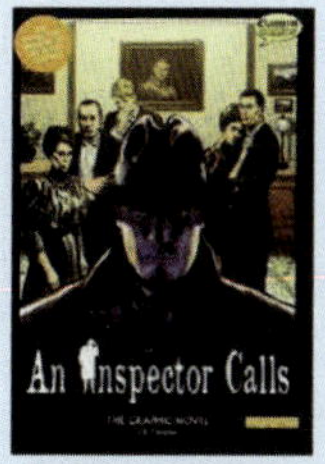	**An Inspector Calls (Original Text)**	This is an intelligently crafted graphic novel adaptation of JB Priestley's dramatic text of the same title. A respectable household is shocked when a strange man visits them shortly after dinner and proceeds to unravel their prejudices and lies. Also available in *Quick Text* version (ISBN 978-1-906332-33-4).	JB Priestley & Jason Cobley	Classical Comics	Classics Literary Adaptation Mystery	9781906332327	2 stars
	**Batman: The Court of Owls**	Gotham City experiences some brutal murders. Batman is soon on the scene and begins to realise that these crimes probably have causes that go back many years. As our Caped Crusader begins to unravel this deadly mystery, he discovers a conspiracy going back to his youth and beyond to the origins of the city he's sworn to protect. The start of a bold new era for *Batman* with a new creative team, this is the first volume in a series that has achieved both huge critical and commercial success…. and introduced a whole new level of mystery to the Gotham mythos.	Scott Snyder & Greg Capullo	DC	Superheroes Crime	9781401235420	3 stars
	**Batman: The Dark Knight Returns**	It is ten years after an aging Batman has retired and Gotham City has sunk deeper into decadence and lawlessness. Now, as his city needs him most, the Dark Knight returns in a blaze of glory, joined by Carrie Kelly, a teenage female Robin… Frank Miller was at the height of his creative powers when he wrote and illustrated this volume, one of Batman's greatest ever stories. It still packs a wallop and is as gut-wrenching as it was when first published in 1986. Every school library should have this one.	Frank Miller	DC	Superheroes Crime	9781563893421	2 stars

	**Batman: Year One**	One of the most important and critically acclaimed Batman adventures ever! Telling the complete dramatic story of Batman's first year fighting crime, this is widely accepted as a comics classic. Written by Frank Miller (*The Dark Knight Returns*), artwork was handled this time by David Mazzucchelli and his classy, minimalist style perfectly matches the "historical" feel of the story. Again, another Batman graphic novel that should find a place in every school library.	Frank Miller & David Mazzucchelli	DC	Superheroes Crime	9781401207526	2 stars
	**Batwoman: Elegy**	Breathtaking, this has mould-breaking artwork and a hard-hitting story that brings us the adventures of a new, gritty and realistic Gotham heroine. Kate Kane's personal life as the daughter of a military man, surviving twin of a hostage tragedy and openly gay woman makes for a story as fascinating as that of her Batman-inspired alter-ego, Batwoman.	Greg Rucka & JH Williams III	DC	Superheroes Crime	9781401231460	2 stars
	**Breath of Bones: A Tale of the Golem**	A British plane crashes down in a Jewish village, sparking a Nazi invasion. Using clay and mud from the river, the villagers bring to life a giant monster to battle for their freedom and future.... Highly moving and innovative, this is something a little bit different to what you might expect from a graphic novel.	Steve Niles & Dave Wachter	Dark Horse	Historical Fiction World War II Monsters	9781616553449	1 star

	**Cold War**	In this text acclaimed comics creator John Byrne gives us MI-6 agent Michael Swann. In Swann's opening adventure, our secret agent is called on to prevent the defection of an important British scientist which would result in Soviet nuclear dominion over the free world... As the title suggests, this is a slice of old-school, cold war intrigue and espionage from the man largely responsible for bringing us the greatest adventures Marvel's *X-Men* and *Fantastic Four* ever saw.	John Byrne	IDW	Historical Fiction Spies Espionage	9781613771778	2 stars
	**Copperhead, Volume 1**	Welcome to Copperhead, a grimy mining town on the edge of a backwater planet. Single mum Clara Bronson is the new sheriff, and on her first day she has to deal with not only a resentful deputy but also a decidedly suspect mining tycoon, a family of alien hillbillies and a massacre.... Science fiction crashes into Wild West to bring us one of the most exciting comics series of 2015.	Jay Faerber & Scott Godlewski	Image	Sci-fi Murder Western	9781632152213	3 stars
	**Daredevil, Volume 1:**	A critically acclaimed revitalisation of *The Man Without Fear*. Daredevil is the blind superhero who battles the criminal underworld during the night... and during the day as attorney Matt Murdock! This graphic novel brought a fresh approach to showing readers how Daredevil "sees" the world with his special radar sense.	Mark Waid & Paolo Rivera	Marvel	Superheroes Disability	9780785152385	3 stars

	**Daredevil: Born Again**	Here is the definitive Daredevil tale! Karen Page, Attorney Matt Murdock's former lover, in return for a drug fix has betrayed his secret identity. Now, our hero must find the strength to take on the Kingpin of Crime. The creators of *Batman: Year One*'s take on Daredevil brought the hero to his knees... and back up again.	Frank Miller & David Mazzucchelli	Marvel	Superheroes Crime	9780785134817	2 stars
	**Dracula (Original Text)**	Bram Stoker's gothic masterpiece was first published in 1897 and has spawned many classic films – so it's high time we had a graphic novel adaptation that is impressively faithful to the original book. Also available in *Quick Text* version (ISBN 978-1-906332-26-6).	Bram Stoker, Jason Cobley & Staz Johnson	Classical Comics	Classics Literary Adaptation Horror Gothic	9781906332259	3 stars
	**Edward Scissorhands: Parts Unknown**	Many will remember the Tim Burton directed 1990 *Edwards Scissorhands* movie that starred Johnny Depp. Set twenty years after the original movie, this is just as tragic and touching as the original story... In a castle just beyond the boundary of a small urban community, a brilliant inventor created Edward Scissorhands... but left him tragically unfinished. Two generations of exile have left Edward digging through abandoned experiments, but once he wakes up a creature best left buried, he discovers he isn't the only one missing a vital piece... now read on!	Kate Leth & Drew Rausch	IDW	Gothic Movies & TV	9781631402609	2 stars
	**Great Expectations (Original Text)**	Exactly what you'd expect from Classical Comics – another graphic novel adaptation of a classic of literature, brought to you with the fullest of respect for the original source material. Also available in *Quick Text* version (ISBN 9781906332112).	Charles Dickens & Jen Green	Classical Comics	Classics Literary Adaptation	9781906332099	1 star

	**Hawkeye: My Life as a Weapon**	Emerging from *The Avengers* and into his first major solo series, our self-made hero Hawkeye (Clint Barton) begins his first major solo series fighting for justice with ex-*Young Avenger* Kate Bishop as his accomplice. SHIELD recruits Clint to intercept a packet of incriminating evidence – before he becomes the most wanted man in the world. This is the book that made Hawkeye more popular than he'd ever been before and won a ton of comics awards for its new take on Marvel's famous archer.	Matt Fraction & David Aja	Marvel	Superheroes Spies	9780785165620	2 stars
	**Injustice: Gods Among Us**	Things in the DC Universe have changed after Superman is tricked into destroying the one thing he loves the most. Now unwilling to let crime go unpunished, the heroes of our world must choose if they are with Superman, or against him. But not every country will submit to his new world order and neither will Superman's greatest threat – Batman!... Written by Tom Taylor (winner of the 2012 Stan Lee Excelsior Award for *Star Wars: Blood Ties*), this is the first volume of the bestselling prequel series to the popular computer game and free-to-pay mobile app.	Tom Taylor & Jheremy Raapack	DC	Superheroes	9781401248437	2 stars
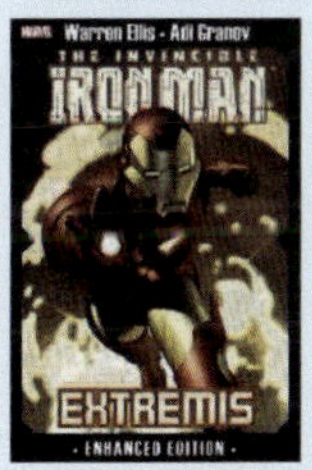	**Iron Man: Extremis**	Here is the story that inspired Marvel Studio's successful film – *Iron Man 3*. It's the beginning of a new era for Iron Man, one that will transform him from a millionaire industrialist in a fancy suit of armour, and into a hero at the forefront of new 21st Century (and beyond!) technologies. There's no going back from the choices Tony Stark makes in *Extremis*.	Warren Ellis & Adi Granov	Marvel	Superheroes Technology	9781846535277	3 stars

	**Jane Eyre (Original text)**	Here is the famous Charlotte Brontë classic transformed by artist John M. Burns. His treatment of Jane Eyre's life nearly two centuries ago is sympathetic and should prove a big success with readers in the same way that the original text succeeds showing the familiar characters and plot. Immerse yourself in this famous love story Also available in *Quick Text* version (ISBN 9781906332082).	Charlotte Bronte, Karen Wenborn & John M. Burns	Classical Comics	Classics Literary Adaptation Love Historical Fiction	9781906332068	1 star
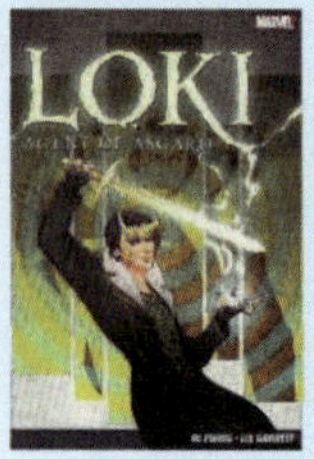	**Loki: Agent of Asgard**	Old God – New Trickster! Kid Loki's is now grown up – and this God of Mischief is stronger sexier and more devious than ever before! Here he is a Asgardia's one-man secret service ready to lie, cheat, steal, bluff and snog his way through the most amazing and most dangerous adventures that the All-Mother can throw at him... starting with a heart-stopping heist on Avengers Tower – and the death of Thor! Full of bare-faced cheek and humour, this will have you reading the character of Loki in Tom Hiddleston's voice.	Al Ewing & Lee Garbett	Marvel	Superheroes Mythology	9781846536007	2 stars
	**Macbeth (Original Text)**	This full colour graphic novel presents Shakespeare's famous "The Scottish Play" just as the author intended: in its original and unabridged format. It is a good introduction to the play for everyone who wants the original text. Witchcraft, superstition, murder – it's all here! Also available in *Plain Text* (ISBN 9781906332044) and *Quick Text* (ISBN 9781906332051).	William Shakespeare & John McDonald	Classical Comics	Classics Shakespeare Tragedy Murder	9781906332037	2 stars

	**Magneto: Testament**	Set in the late 1930's early 40's this wartime story follows Max Eisenhardt as he struggles to protect his family and Magda, a Romani girl, from the indignities of a Nuremberg school, the horrors of Nazi occupied Poland and the atrocities of the infamous concentration camp – Auschwitz-Birkenau. This is as historically based and emotionally charged as you might imagine as it looks at the childhood of one of the most popular *X-Men* characters. It also features in-depth endnotes and extras providing further historical context, including a useful teachers' guide.	Greg Pak & Carmine De Giandomenico	Marvel	Superheroes Historical Fiction Holocaust	9780785191728	2 stars
	**Manga Shakespeare: Hamlet**	This is Shakespeare modernised for 21st Century readers! This version of *Hamlet* is abridged but uses original Shakespearean dialogue and text. We now live in an ever divided world, separate colonies have emerged and the state of Denmark is successful and prosperous – but is it? The founding family is wealthy but this has come at a price – corruption. It could be that the greatest threat of all comes from within the walls of Elsinore itself rather than from neighbouring states… As with all of the *Manga Shakespeare* series, this was produced in the UK and so keeps the traditional left-to-right format that UK readers are used to, unlike traditional Japanese manga that is produced right-to-left.	William Shakespeare & Emma Vieceli	SelfMadeHero	Classics Shakespeare Tragedy	9780955285615	2 stars

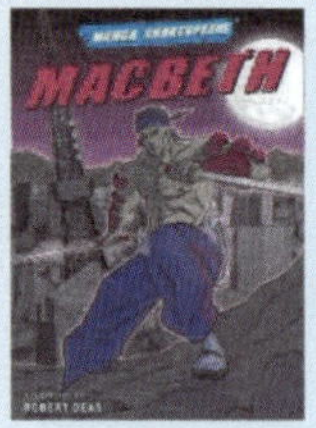	**Manga Shakespeare: Macbeth**	Macbeth as not often seen – Samurai warriors have reclaimed a future post-nuclear world of mutants in this manga version of Shakespeare's familiar story of royal treachery and intrigue. Abridged but keeping true to Shakespeare's original text and the manga style makes it accessible for students and is an ideal way of getting to grips with the themes in *Macbeth* and Shakespeare's other plays.	William Shakespeare & Robert Deas	SelfMadeHero	Classics Shakespeare Sci-fi Dystopia Tragedy	9780955285660	3 stars
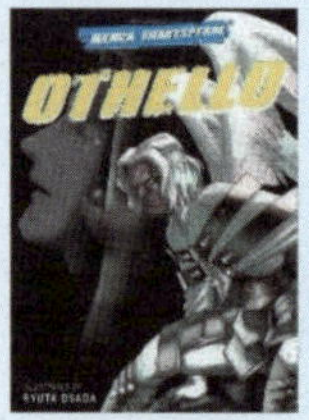	**Manga Shakespeare: Othello**	Another well know Shakespeare favourite. This one begins in a Venetian street and quickly shows the grudges and passionate jealousies that follow. Here Othello's misfortunate plot is quickly revealed in this fantastical, and successful manga version of the classic story.	William Shakespeare & Ryuta Osada	SelfMadeHero	Classics Shakespeare Tragedy Fantasy	9780955816956	2 stars
	**Manga Shakespeare: Richard III**	Richard III good king or bad? As we know, Shakespeare's famous history play reveals the power of the 'dark side'. The series keeps to the language of Shakespeare, but the text is specially abridged for use in the manga. This adaptation succeeds in revealing the possible blackness of this king finally discovered under a Leicester car park – or was it simply effective Tudor propaganda?	William Shakespeare & Patrick Warren	SelfMadeHero	Classics Shakespeare History Murder	9780955285639	2 stars
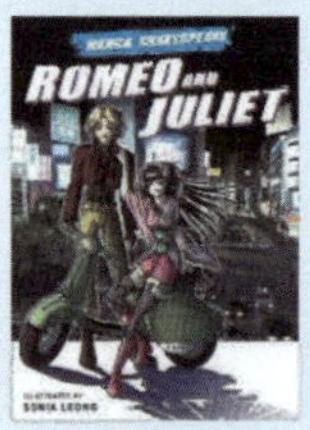	**Manga Shakespeare: Romeo and Juliet**	Removed from Italy to modern Tokyo, with the Capulets and Montagues recast as organised-crime rivals here is the famous story. Abridged enough to move quickly without sacrificing content or meaning, this racy retelling centres on the doomed love story and the foolish rivalry that shapes it. Included is a useful plot summary and the opening colour pages with the cast of characters will help readers follow the story. Perfect for students studying *Romeo and Juliet* at GCSE.	William Shakespeare & Sonia Leong	SelfMadeHero	Classics Shakespeare Tragedy Family Love	9780955285608	3 stars

	**Manga Shakespeare: The Merchant of Venice**	One of Shakespeare's greatest and, in recent years, most controversial plays focusing, as it does, on the spiteful Jewish money-lender Shylock. Faye Yong transforms Venice into a fantastical floating city full of beautiful Elves. A good read for young students.	William Shakespeare & Faye Yong	SelfMadeHe ro	Classics Shakespeare Tragedy Fantasy	9780955816918	2 stars
	**Manga Shakespeare: Twelfth Night**	Here is another Shakespeare favourite accessible for all in this attractive format. Here is the author's familiar tale of unrequited love, family dispute and a fatal shipwreck. At the beginning of the story, everyone is alone; by the end, everyone – well, almost everyone – has found their other half. Equal parts mysterious, romantic and humorous, this adaptation is a wonderful use of the manga medium.	William Shakespeare & Nana Li	SelfMadeHe ro	Classics Shakespeare Comedy Love	9780955816994	2 stars
	**Maus**	The Pulitzer Prize-winning *Maus* tells the story of Vladek Spiegelman, a Jewish survivor of Hitler's Europe, and his son, a cartoonist coming to terms with his father's story. *Maus* uses the comic form to represent the Nazis as cats and the Jews as their mice victims, shocking readers out of any lingering sense of familiarity with the Holocaust and everything it represents about humanity. Regarded by many comics historians, academics and readers as the greatest graphic novel of all time, this is not an easy read... but nor should it be.	Art Spiegelman	Penguin	World War II Holocaust	9780141014081	1 star

	**Moonhead and the Music Machine**	Life is a peach when you have a moon for a head. Your head can wander out of the atmosphere into galactic reveries, roll lazily into jungles or soar closer than Icarus to the sun's seething glare. Snap! Back in reality, the world of a teenage boy is a much crueller place. And when the school talent contest takes its yearly turn, it is the role of the outcast to take part. An imaginative and visually poetic take on the stock American high school drama.... this wonderfully psychedelic and beautifully presented book succeeds in making the reader celebrate the typical "high school loner" instead of just pitying them. A clever study of the transformative power of music and friendship.	Andrew Rae	Nobrow	Humour School Life	9781907704789	2 stars
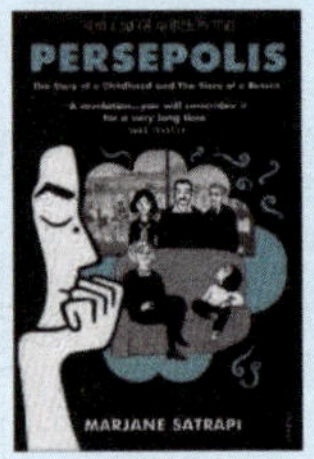	**Persepolis**	The semi-autobiographical account of the author's childhood growing up in Iran as the daughter of Marxist parents, *Persepolis* paints an unforgettable portrait of daily life in Iran and of the bewildering contradictions between home life and public life. Presented in a simplistic and monochromatic style, *Persepolis* excludes nobody from its story. You don't need a love of politics and a radical conscience to love *Persepolis*.	Marjane Satrapi	Vintage	Multicultural Autobiography	9780099523994	1 star
	**Peter Panzerfaust, Volume 1: The Great Escape**	Put simply this is a reinvention of JM Barrie's classic *Peter Pan* story but placed in the context of occupied France in World War II. A coming-of-age tale told through the eyes of a group of French orphans who are saved by a brave, daring and mysterious American boy named Peter. Set in a travel through France that involves the French Resistance and fighting a fanatical SS officer determined to destroy them, this is an action packed thriller. Great for readers who loved *Peter Pan* and for readers who love stories set in WWII.	Kurtis J. Wiebe & Tyler Jenkins	Image	World War II	9781607065821	2 stars

	**Predator Omnibus, Volume 1**	Dark Horse took the comics industry by storm (again!) with its first *Predator* comics in 1989, a series that captured the gripping and fearsome feel of the films it was based upon. This value-for-money, 400-page omnibus edition features the first three Dark Horse *Predator* series – *Concrete Jungle*, *Cold War* and *Dark River* – in full colour.	Mark Verheiden et al	Dark Horse	Sci-fi Horror Movies & TV	9781593077327	3 stars
	**Predator: Prey to the Heavens**	Amidst a brutal third-world civil war, Earth has become the setting for conflict between two tribes attempting to destroy each other. Each is the other's prey, each the other's Predator. Thrilling but violent – just what you'd expect from a *Predator* graphic novel.	John Arcudi & Javier Saltares	Dark Horse	Sci-fi Horror Movies & TV	9781595824929	3 stars
	**Quantum and Woody, Volume 1: The World's Worst Superhero Team**	Once upon a time, Eric and Woody Henderson were inseparable. Adopted brothers. Best friends. Brilliant minds. Years later, they are estranged siblings, petty rivals, and washed-up failures. But when their father's murder leads them into the throes of a life-altering scientific accident, Eric and Woody will find themselves with a whole new purpose – and a perfectly legitimate reason to wear costumes and fight crime...! Absolutely hilarious, this buddy superhero tale sails very close to the wind on occasion but was so popular with UK teens that it finished runner-up in the 2014 Stan Lee Excelsior Award with a score that would have won it any other year!	James Asmus & Tom Fowler	Valiant	Superheroes Humour	9781939346186	3 stars

	**Red Sonja: She-Devil with a Sword Omnibus, Volume 1**	This massive omnibus features 19 issues of the hit series that re-introduced Red Sonja to today's audiences. Experience an impressive 464 pages of top-rate sword and sorcery action! Swords, wizards, monsters and a strong female lead character (who isn't just titillation) combine to create a believable fantasy world.	Michael Avon Oeming, Mike Carey & Mel Rubi	Dynamite	Fantasy	9781606901014	2 stars
	**Rime of the Ancient Mariner**	The great narrative ballad written by Samuel Taylor Coleridge, rendered as a comic book by Hunt Emerson. A great way to get to grips with this classic of English Literature and have a little fun along the way.	Samuel Taylor Coleridge & Hunt Emerson	Knockabout	Classics Literary Adaptation Cartoon	9780861660650	1 star
	**Romeo and Juliet (Original Text)**	This is the full and unabridged play as a graphic novel! Shakespeare's tragic tale of doomed love and feuding families is perhaps his most famous creation and this adaptation has a very Shakespearean visual style. Also available in *Plain Text* (ISBN 9781906332204) and *Quick Text* (ISBN 9781906332211).	William Shakespeare & John McDonald	Classical Comics	Classics Shakespeare Tragedy	9781906332198	2 stars
	**Sally Heathcote: Suffragette**	*Sally Heathcote: Suffragette* is a gripping inside story of the campaign for votes for women. A tale of loyalty, love and courage, set against a vividly realised backdrop of Edwardian Britain, it follows the fortunes of a maid-of-all-work swept up in the feminist militancy of the era….. A beautifully presented hardback book with soft, minimally coloured artwork, Sally Heathcote is a very easy character to respect, love and admire.	Mary Talbot, Bryan Talbot & Kate Charlesworth	Jonathan Cape	Historical Fiction	9780224097864	1 star

	**Sweeney Todd: The Demon Barber of Fleet Street**	Here is the familiar story retold for a new audience. From his barber shop in Fleet Street, Sweeney Todd murders selected customers to steal their money and valuables. Some suspect he is up to no good, but no one knows how he actually kills his victims. How does he dispose of the bodies? And what is his connection with Mrs. Lovett who runs a popular pie shop nearby? Illustrated by regular Marvel artist Declan Shalvey (from Ireland), this book presents the full horror of Todd's life and world without resorting to anything gory or gratuitous. Also available in *Quick Text* (ISBN 9781906332808).	Sean Michael Wilson & Declan Shalvey	Classical Comics	Literary Adaptation Murder Historical Fiction	9781906332792	2 stars
	**The Delinquents**	Quantum & Woody, Archer & Armstrong are the Delinquents! Circumstances dictate that these ill-suited and irresponsible "heroes" get involved in a cross-country race through the darkest corners of American mythology – chaos ensues… Full of irreverent humour and personality clashes, *The Delinquents* is a surprisingly fun read with more than a few creative indulgences along the way.	James Asmus, Fred Van Lente & Kano	Valiant	Humour Adventure	9781939346513	1 star

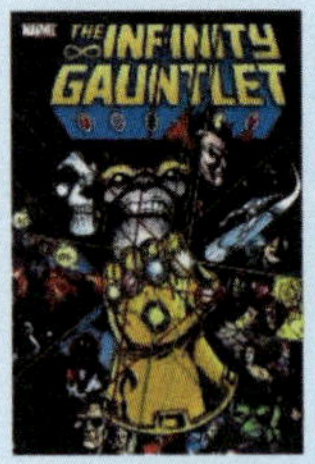	**The Infinity Gauntlet**	The epic tale of cosmic power and destruction that included nearly all of Marvel's superheroes in their struggle against the mad Thanos (see recent Marvel movies for his string-pulling cameos), this story forms the basis of the *Avengers: Infinity War* movies scheduled for release in 2018 and 2019. The Infinity Gauntlet is Marvel's "Holy Grail". With it comes omnipotence: the absolute control of all aspects of time, space, power, reality, the mind, and the soul. And Thanos doesn't want to control the universe… he wants to kill everything in it.	Jim Starlin & Ron Lim	Marvel	Superheroes Cosmic	9780785156598	3 stars
	**The Legend of Drizzt, Volume 1: Homeland**	The young prince of a royal house, Drizzt Do'Urden grows to maturity in the vile world of the Dark Elves. Possessing honour beyond the scope of his unprincipled society, young Drizzt faces an inevitable dilemma. Can he live in a world that rejects integrity? A graphic novel adaptation of RA Salvatore's bestselling novels based on the *Forgotten Realms* role-playing games. This is the first volume in a trilogy that will see Drizzt leave his wicked kin behind, carve a life for himself where he doesn't have to indulge in acts of unspeakable evil and eventually find his way to the surface world.	RA Salvatore, Andrew Dabb & Tim Seeley	IDW	Fantasy	9781631401978	2 stars

	**Thor, Volume 1: Goddess of Thunder**	The great hammer Mjolnir lies on the moon, unable to be lifted by anyone in all the heavens! Even Thor! Something dark has befallen the God of Thunder, leaving him weakened and for the first time... unworthy! But when Frost Giants invade the Earth, the hammer will be lifted and an all-new Thor will arise! A Thor unlike any we've ever seen before! Who is this new Goddess of Thunder? Not even Odin knows...! People laughed when the notion of a “gender change” for one of Marvel’s most famous and masculine characters was first mooted. That was over a year ago and people aren’t laughing anymore. Jason Aaron has put together a story of ancient Norse gods and an unprincipled international energy company – with large slices of fantasy and mystery thrown in – that has been one of Marvel’s best comics series for a while now. Jump on board for the adventures of the female Thor!	Jason Aaron & Russell Dauterman	Marvel	Superheroes Mythology Magic	9781846536564	4 stars
	**Wolverine: Origin**	A fantastic and yet heart-breaking tale of Wolverine’s early childhood days growing up on his rich parents’ plantation in late 19th Century Canada – until family tragedy strikes and he is set on the path that will lead him to manifest his mutation and everything that comes after that. This is not the Wolverine origin story that you expected.	Paul Jenkins & Andy Kubert	Marvel	Historical Fiction	9781904159070	2 stars
	**Wolverine: Weapon X**	What is Wolverine? – this depends on who you are, but to one infamous group he was but a weapon – that kills. Find out for yourself in this *X-Men* prequel graphic novel with revelations of the murderous mysteries that have shaped Wolverine’s life, a life even he doesn’t fully remember. A useful and popular read	Barry Windsor-Smith	Marvel	Superheroes	9780785137269	2 stars

	**Wonder Woman: Blood**	Hippolyta, Queen of the Amazons and mother to Wonder Woman, has kept a secret from her daughter all her life – but when Wonder Woman discovers the true identity of her father her life will sink into chaos and confusion. Steeped in ancient Greek mythology but placed in a very modern superhero setting, *Wonder Woman: Blood* is a bold new direction that surprised and enthralled readers when it debuted in 2012.	Brian Azzarello & Cliff Chiang	DC	Superheroes Mythology	9781401235628	3 stars
	**Wuthering Heights (Original Text)**	Emily Brontë's only novel is famous the world over. This is a masterpiece of classical literature. Hardship, insanity, cruelty, frustrated love, and ghosts – all the ingredients of a brilliant read. With each page hand-painted by highly respected UK comics artist John M. Burns, this is a graphic novel adaptation than can take your breath away with its detail and its beauty. Also available in *Quick Text* (ISBN 9781906332884).	Emily Brontë & John M. Burns	Classical Comics	Classics Literary Adaptations Love Tragedy	9781906332877	1 star
	**Wolverine & The X-Men (Marvel Noir)**	In 2009, Marvel presented a new range of graphic novels – *Marvel Noir* – that mixed their traditional superhero universe with elements of *film noir* and *pulp fiction* to create a new, darker, grittier, hard-boiled world set in the 1930s and 1940s. These aren't superhero stories – but fans of these characters will recognise strong elements of the Marvel universe amongst the pages. This book features the *X-Men Noir* and *Wolverine Noir* stories. Other characters covered in this interesting move included Iron Man, Deadpool, Spider-Man and The Punisher.	Fred Van Lente & Dennis Calero	Marvel	Superheroes Noir Fiction Detectives	9780785183822	2 stars

16+

Cover	Title	Description	Creators	Publisher	Genre	ISBN	Lendability 4 stars max.
	**100 Bullets**	This dark and intriguing Eisner Award-winning series features a mysterious agent named Graves who approaches ordinary citizens and gives them an opportunity to exact revenge on a person who has wronged them. Offering his clients an attaché case containing proof of the deed and a gun with untraceable bullets, he guarantees his "clients" full immunity for all of their actions – including murder…! This volume collects the first 19 issues. Strong crime fiction and a deep, deep mystery combine to grab readers by the lapels and force them to ask themselves what they would do with Graves' 100 bullets.	Brian Azzarello & Eduardo Risso	DC	Crime Revenge Mystery	9781401250560	2 stars
	**300**	It is 480 BC and the Persian armies of King Xerxes have advanced to the very frontiers of diminutive and politically fragmented Greece. Standing between Greece and this presumed tidal wave of destruction is a tiny detachment of but three hundred warriors. This is Frank Miller's (*Batman: Year One*, *The Dark Knight Returns*, *Daredevil: Born Again*) epic retelling of history's supreme moment of battlefield valour. A physically-long graphic novel (not in page count but if you own it, you'll know what I mean!) that has since been made famous by Zack Snyder's ground-breaking 2007 movie of the same name. This is a glorious hardback edition with wonderfully deep colouring.	Frank Miller & Lynn Varley	Dark Horse	Mythology War	9781569714027	3 stars

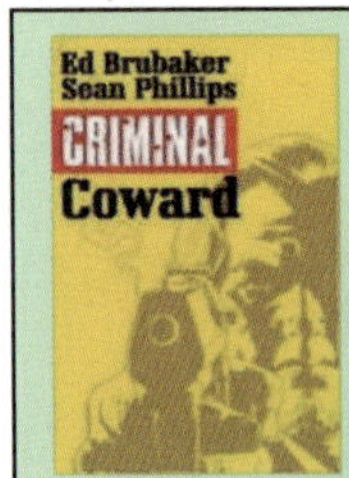	**Criminal, Volume 1: Coward**	Meet Leo, who can plan the perfect heist… but only if he can be convinced the job is safe enough. See, Leo is a professional. So when an old friend and a crooked cop approach him with a plan to hold up an evidence transport van, Leo must make some tough choices… knowing that there's nothing you can trust less than a cop on the take. The first volume in Ed Brubaker's and Sean Philips' crime fiction masterpieces. Brubaker, in particular, has since gone on to be widely recognised as one of the best writers in comics today (see his other series *Velvet*, *The Fade Out* and *Fatale*).	Ed Brubaker & Sean Phillips	Icon	Crime	9781632151704	2 stars
	**Death: Deluxe Edition**	The first story – *Death: The High Cost of Living* – introduces the young, pale, perky, and genuinely likable Death. One day in every century, Death walks the Earth to better understand those to whom she will be the final visitor. Today is that day. What follows is a sincere musing on love, life and (of course) death. In the second story – *Death: The Time of Your Life* – a rising star of the music world wrestles with revealing her true sexual orientation just as her lover is lured into the realm of Death. A practical, honest, and intelligent story that illuminates "the miracle of death". Wonderful and touching stories by much-loved author Neil Gaiman that will be loved by all the "Goth girls" in your school… as well as many of the boys. Thought-provoking and illustrated in a sweet style that belies the potentially depressing nature of the subject material.	Neil Gaiman & Chris Bachalo	DC	Supernatural Fantasy	9781401235482	2 stars
	**Defoe: 1666**	London 1668 – -it is two years since the city was devastated by the Great Fire, the inferno caused by a comet passing over the capital – but from the ashes rose the undead, hungry for the flesh of the living… Originally published in UK weekly comic anthology *2000AD*, this is the "real" story of the Great Fire of London that the history books don't tell you!	Pat Mills & Leigh Gallagher	Rebellion/ 2000AD	Historical Fiction Zombies	9781906735104	2 stars

	**East of West**	*East of West* is a science fiction Western set in a future dystopian version of the United States where the Civil War never really ended. The fate of this warped vision of America rests with... the Four Horsemen of the Apocalypse. One of the most critically acclaimed and bestselling comics series of recent years. Personally speaking, Jonathan Hickman is probably my favourite current comics writer. His breadth of vision is astounding. Hickman plays the long game!	Jonathan Hickman & Nick Dragotta	Image	Supernatural Occult Post-Apocalyptic	9781607067702	1 star
	**Grandville**	In *Grandville*, the first volume in the series, legendary UK comics creator Bryan Talbot brings us his anthropomorphic, steampunk masterpiece. It tells the story of Detective Inspector LeBrock of Scotland Yard as he stalks a gang of murderers through the heart of Belle Époque Paris. In this alternative reality, France is the major world power and its capital throngs with steam-driven hansom cabs, automatons and flying machines.... and is populated by a huge variety of talking animals! *Grandville* will be popular with younger students too but it is down to your personal preference whether you will consider it suitable for them.	Bryan Talbot	Jonathan Cape	Mystery Steampunk Animals	9780224084888	4 stars
	**Hellboy: Seed of Destruction**	*Hellboy* has been one of the most celebrated comics series of the last 20 years. A demonic supernatural investigator pulled from Hell as a child by Nazi occultists in World War II, Hellboy has captured the imagination of comics readers of all ages, with his striking visual image allowing him to breakthrough into the worlds of movies and video games with ease. Taking inspiration from folk tales, pulp fiction and horror stories, Mike Mignola never seems to run out of new stories for his eponymous hero. This is the first of twelve volumes of *Hellboy*, although the character features in more stories than just his own series.	Mike Mignola & John Byrne	Dark Horse	Supernatural Occult Mystery	9781593070946	2 stars

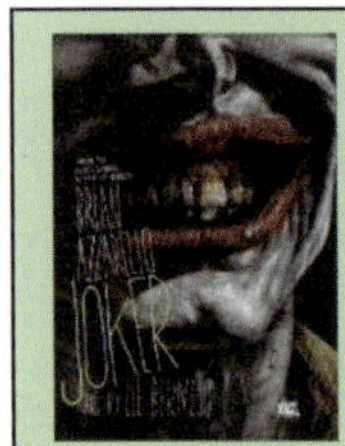	**Joker**	After another stint in the Elizabeth Arkham Asylum for the Criminally Insane, the Joker finds his city of Gotham divided between rival gangs of mobsters and costumed villains. Not content to let this happen, the Joker determines to change things. Enter some of Gotham's most wanted, including Two-Face, The Riddler, Killer Croc, Penguin, Harley Quinn and even Batman himself! Darkly compelling and somewhat disturbing in places, this has more in common with movies like *Good Fellas* and *The Godfather* than it does with traditional *Batman* stories. Extremely good stuff by the writer of *100 Bullets* though.	Brian Azzarello & Lee Bermejo	DC	Crime Gangsters	9781401215811	3 stars
	**Lazarus, Volume 1**	In an apparently hopeless dystopian future of near economic collapse, governments have become obsolete and everything is owned and ruled by a handful of families, who jealously guard what privilege they have and exploit the masses as disposable workers and cattle. Forever Carlyle, our heroine, defends her family's holdings through deception and force as their Lazarus, their protector. Shot dead defending the family home, Forever Carlyle's day goes downhill from there... Grim, moody and atmospheric, this is *The Hunger Games* for readers who prefer their dystopian fiction to be a little more... desperate.	Greg Rucka & Michael Lark	Image	Dystopia	9781607068099	2 stars
	**Palestine**	In the early 1990s, journalist and comics creator Joe Sacco spent two months in the West Bank and Gaza Strip – travelling, talking to Palestinians and recording all his experiences in his notebooks. Upon returning to the United States he started writing and drawing *Palestine*, a ground-breaking graphic novel that perfectly combines the techniques of eyewitness reportage with the medium of comic-book storytelling. Sacco highlights the history and plight of the Palestinian people (as a group and as individuals) in a way that doesn't overtly point the finger of blame and invites readers to use their humanity to reach their own conclusions.	Joe Sacco	Jonathan Cape	Non-fiction Reportage	9780224069823	2 stars

	**Pride of Baghdad**	It is 2003. In the shadow of the Gulf War and to the consternation of many, a pride of lions escapes from Baghdad Zoo during an American bombing raid. Free at last, lost, confused and inevitably hungry, these four lions roam the decimated streets of Baghdad. *Pride of Baghdad* raises questions about the true meaning of liberation – can it be given, or is it earned only through self-determination and sacrifice? The escaped animals provide a disturbing metaphor for the Iraqi people. This fantastic graphic novel encourages readers to ask whether better to die free than to live in captivity.	Brian K. Vaughan & Niko Henrichon	DC	Satire War Animals	9781401203153	2 stars
	**The Sandman, Volume 1: Preludes and Nocturnes**	An occultist attempting to capture Death, to bargain for eternal life, traps Death's younger brother Morpheus (Lord of Dreams) instead. After his 70-year imprisonment and eventual escape, Morpheus goes on a quest for his lost objects of power. On his arduous journey, Morpheus encounters Lucifer, John Constantine and an all-powerful madman. This book also includes the story "The Sound of Her Wings" which introduces the character of Death. This is the first volume of Neil Gaiman's long-running comics masterpiece – a series that, perhaps more than any other, showed the world that comics could be for adults and could have genuine and real philosophical and spiritual depth.	Neil Gaiman et al	DC	Supernatural Occult Fantasy	9781401225759	2 stars

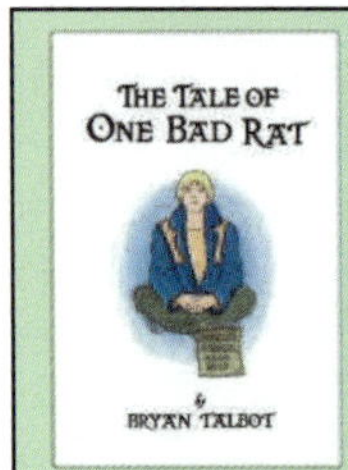	**The Tale of One Bad Rat**	*The Tale of One Bad Rat* is the story of a teenage girl who runs away from home to escape an uncaring mother and a sexually abusive father. Eventually, she finds herself drawn to the Lake District by her love of the works of Beatrix Potter, and in that beautiful landscape she begins to accept her past, build a new life for herself… and confront her parents. A genuine classic of the comics medium, *The Tale of One Bad Rat* is drawn in a simple, naturalistic style with hand-painted colours. Unusually for comics, all of the characters are drawn from life, and the locations from photographs of real places.	Bryan Talbot	Jonathan Cape	Family Abuse	9780224084703	2 stars
	**The Walking Dead, Volume 1: Days Gone Bye**	Launched in 2003, this black-and-white comic book series is still issuing new monthly stories today! What could easily be pigeon-holed as a straightforward tale of human survival in a zombie apocalypse, actually has a level of humanity and a sense of bleakness that sucks in readers and has made *The Walking Dead* a sales phenomenon over the last ten years. The lack of colour and the consistency of the writer/artist team has created a world that readers can keep identifying with and feel a part of… even if they can't guarantee the longevity of any of the characters! It is currently up to 25 volumes and whilst the collected omnibuses might provide better value for money they are of a size that might provide problems for libraries.	Robert Kirkman & Tony Moore	Image	Zombies Horror Post-Apocalyptic	9781582406725	4 stars

	**V For Vendetta**	*V for Vendetta* is a powerful read – a story about loss of freedom and individuality. Taking place in a totalitarian England following a devastating war that changed the face of the planet, this is a world without political freedom, personal freedom and precious little faith in anything. Enter a mysterious man in a white porcelain mask who fights political oppressors through terrorism and seemingly absurd acts. It's a gripping tale of the blurred lines between ideological good and evil… It's difficult to know what other superlatives to add here. *V for Vendetta* is my favourite graphic novel of all time and I struggle to be fully objective about it. Put simply, if you've ever felt disillusioned or oppressed by the political and class systems in the UK, then you will almost certainly enjoy this book.	Alan Moore & David Lloyd	DC	Thriller Dystopia Politics	9781401208417	4 stars
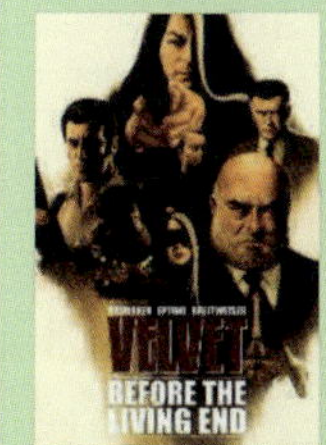	**Velvet, Volume 1: Before The Living End**	When the world's greatest secret agent is killed, all evidence points to Velvet Templeton, the personal secretary to the Director of the Agency. But Velvet's got a dark secret buried in her past... because she's also the most dangerous woman alive... Set in the 1970s, *Velvet* is steeped in a classic *James Bond* style that fans of Sean Connery and Roger Moore will recognise and love. It is much darker than their family-friendly *Bond* movies though and closer to Ian Fleming's original ideas of how secret agents work in the Cold War era.	Ed Brubaker & Steve Epting	Image	Spies Thriller	9781607069645	2 stars

	**Watchmen**	Widely regarded as the greatest graphic novel ever produced, it is no exaggeration to describe *Watchmen* as a work of genius… In an alternate world where the mere presence of American superheroes changed history, the US won the Vietnam War, Nixon is still president, and the Cold War is in full effect. *Watchmen* begins as a murder-mystery, but soon unfolds into a planet-altering conspiracy. As the resolution comes to a head, the unlikely group of reunited heroes – Rorschach, Nite Owl, Silk Spectre, Dr. Manhattan and Ozymandias – have to test the limits of their convictions and ask themselves where the true line is between good and evil. Multi-layered and multi-styled storytelling coupled with more traditional comics artwork and structured by both writer and artist with such precision, this book will change your preconceptions of what can be done with the superhero genre.	Alan Moore & Dave Gibbons	DC	Superheroes Alternate Earth Murder Mystery Conspiracy	9781401248192	4 stars
	**Y: The Last Man, Book 1**	Imagine being the only male human survivor of a planet-wide plague that instantly kills every mammal possessing a Y chromosome! Yorick Brown, accompanied by a mysterious government agent, a brilliant young geneticist and his pet monkey travels the world in search of his lost love and to discover why he's the last man on Earth. However, being the only male human left makes him a target for a wide variety of groups and individuals… and leads to a life full of threats and dangers. From the same writer as *Pride of Baghdad*, this comic series was collected into ten paperback volumes or five hardback deluxe editions.	Brian K. Vaughan & Pia Guerra	DC	Post-Apocalyptic Survival Mystery	9781401251512	2 stars

Index of Titles

Index of Creators